THE
SERMON
ON THE
MOUNT

THE
SERMON
ON THE
MOUNT

A Guide for Practical Faith

Jason Martin

Mennonite Publishing House
Scottdale, Pennsylvania

MENNONITE PUBLISHING HOUSE
Scottdale, Pa. 15683

© 1986 by Mennonite Publishing House.
All rights reserved. Published 1986.
Printed in the United States of America.
Designer: Gwen M. Stamm
Library of Congress Catalog Card Number: 86-61453

Contents

Foreword

Without doubt, the most powerful sermon ever preached was the Sermon on the Mount. Regardless of whether it was presented all in one setting or later pulled together as a composite sermon from the whole range of Jesus' teachings, it remains in all its beauty and power. It penetrates to the heart of what it means to be human, and how we can enter into the fullness of the human experience.

The radical vision of love in the Sermon on the Mount is lofty. Who can attain it? No wonder that so many interpreters of the Sermon have explained it away. Some say that although individual human beings should allow the Sermon to influence their personal lives, it is an illusion to think that the church and state could live up to it (classical Lutheranism). Others see it as an ideal toward which church and state should slowly work, step by step, hoping for an ever purer and more godly church and Christian society (classical Calvinism). Still others allow for a small number within their midst to commit themselves to this high ideal, saying that for the masses within the established church it would be an impossible ideal to live up to (Roman Catholicism). Then there are those who declare that the Sermon is null and void for the current Christian era and that it will come into its own only in a later dispensation (the view of some dispensationalists). Finally, most people view the Sermon as simply a lofty pattern, not meant to be entered into and lived out in all of its dimensions, but simply to be there as an incentive—to go one step in the right direction.

Yet who in his or her right mind could be so bold as to say, "I intend to live out the Sermon on the Mount"? The Anabaptists were so bold! When asked by state-church representatives on what basis they could claim to be obedient disciples of Jesus as defined in the Sermon on the Mount, they invariably would respond: Humanly speaking, it is impossible of course. Yet Jesus commands us as his disciples to live out our lives in this "Sermon manner"; and we respond, deeply desiring to be obedient. And God strengthens each of us as we respond in obedience to his call.

The Anabaptists also invariably added one other thought: Discipleship as defined by the Sermon on the Mount can be lived only within the gathered community of the faithful, where the spirit of the Prince of Peace is present.

Mennonites traditionally have made the Sermon on the Mount the substance defining their faith. Here are the "Ten Commandments" of the New Testament, so named by writers such as Benjamin Eby—writing from Berlin (Kitchener), Ontario, in 1841—who views the Sermon as the true doctrinal center of Jesus Christ, along with the need for repentance (4:17), the great commandment (22:37-39), and the great commission (28:19). Benjamin Eby then attempts, historically, to show how the Mennonites had been continuing the discipleship and kingdom-of-God tradition, as part of God's people, throughout the centuries.

Jason Martin, the author of this fine study guide and interpretation of the Sermon on the Mount, represents the best of the Anabaptist-Mennonite tradition, which considers the Sermon the fundamental definition of discipleship. Each generation of Christians needs to come afresh to the Sermon on the Mount. Martin brings a relevance and freshness in his approach to the "first Christian sermon." His approach to interpretation and his call to renewed obedience are set consciously within the arena of the human complexities of the 1980s.

Once again we need to look at this great foundation and source of our discipleship. It is as great a reality for our day as it was in Jesus' day. And just as Jesus was not afraid to speak to those most difficult issues of all—human relationships—so also Jason Martin, who courageously sets the Sermon within the improbable context of the last decades of the twentieth century.

Yes, it is again time for groups to gather around the Word as presented by Jesus in the Sermon on the Mount. These teachings— given their truly radical meaning—continue to make sense to such groups as the Mennonites, Quakers, and Brethren. They are also being picked up in all their radical fullness by many believers of Catholic and classical Protestant traditions.

If the whole world would come to know and live out the Sermon on the Mount, then there would indeed be no war anymore and the lion would lie down with the lamb. Cannot at least the church of Jesus Christ continue to proclaim this message—by living out the Sermon—the essence of what it means to be Christian?

—Leonard Gross
Goshen, Indiana

Preface

Variety is a new and valuable approach to congregational curriculum materials. Many a church's approach to Christian education is in remarkable contrast to that of thirty years ago, when everyone used the Uniform Series quarterly. It is even more startling to compare today with, say, 1850, when all congregations had was a two-hour Sunday morning worship service—in some places only every other Sunday at that.

This study of the Sermon on the Mount takes advantage of the new freedom to study different materials. However, it has a deeper purpose than adding to the variety of curriculum materials. It is also offered as a corrective to the weakness of book studies that involve only indirect Bible study. Here the goal is to develop direct, personal involvement with the Bible.

My second goal in writing this material is personal. For years I struggled to find my way between theology divorced from practice on the one hand and practice without careful theological reflection on the other. In my struggle, the Sermon on the Mount became the answer. It gave me a sense of direction that I found healing, helpful, and as up-to-date as the morning paper or the evening network news. The latter confuse me; the Sermon fuses me. I am interested in motivating other people to mix minds with the Sermon on the Mount, hoping that they will emerge with a new mind-set—with a serious commitment to live by the Lord's will, which is so intently presented in three chapters of Matthew.

The Sermon on the Mount is prime agenda for me. It helps me to manage my affairs both public and private. It is native ground. By keeping it I find fulfillment of the orientation given me in the Mennonite Church. It also builds on the groundwork laid down in my life by the redeeming ministry of Jesus Christ.

The Sermon on the Mount is thus also the agenda for the Mennonite Church—and other churches for that matter. I find people ready to hear and respond to these moral and ethical guidelines from Jesus. It should be preached, studied, and taught so as to show the clear direction that it can give through the rampant moral confusion in our society.

In a confused time, people need both the good news of the redemptive cross of Christ and the refreshing moral and ethical standards of the Sermon on the Mount. But, regrettably, they are more likely to hear only about the cross, without the call to make the difficult moral decisions that Jesus spoke to. The gospel has nowhere been more stripped and emasculated than in regard to the Sermon on the Mount. Far too many people have ruled its influence out of their lives. Some, like Luther, say it cannot apply to public life. Other interpreters water it down in other ways. Here are seven views of the Sermon on the Mount as summarized from C. F. H. Henry (*Christian Personal Ethics* [Grand Rapids, Mich.: William B. Eerdmans, 1957]):

1. *Humanistic.* Humanists sever the Sermon from the supernatural and from human sinfulness. They view it as an ancient ethical code that is inadequate for the complexities of modern life.

2. *Liberal.* Essentially, liberals interpret the Sermon as offering salvation by human works. They do not highly value salvation as a gift of God's grace. Salvation is dependent on personal fulfillment of the ethical requirements of the Sermon.

3. *Dispensational.* To dispensationalists the Sermon has no relevance for today. It is intended for an age of righteousness, for the future millennial rule of Christ, not the present age ruled by Satan. It is only law and contains no gospel. To dispensationalists

the kingdom of heaven and the kingdom of God are not the same.

4. *Interim ethic.* Albert Schweitzer and others held that Jesus expected the world to end very soon and gave the Sermon as the way to live in that brief interim period. It is impractical over the long haul.

5. *Existential.* Existentialists have held that the value of the Sermon is in producing right attitudes rather than right conduct. The Sermon does not give concrete ethical instructions but is valid for everyone who shares the mind and attitude that the Sermon illustrates. The Sermon convicts us of moral failure to prod us on to ethical obedience.

6. *Anabaptist-Mennonite.* The Sermon is to be obeyed in all areas of life—personal, social, business, and political. It outlines the morality which distinguishes the regenerate believers. It is to be understood in the normal sense of language used in a literal way. It is the New Testament code for all relationships.

7. *Reformed.* Historic Reformed theology holds that the Sermon presents the deeper implications of moral law. It demonstrates the practical way that love is expressed in daily conduct. Its intention is the same as that of Old Testament law—that it be obeyed. Reformed theology stressed the similarity between the Sermon on the Mount and Old Testament law. But its application is only in person-to-person relations. Hence, it does not speak to questions of war or the oath of truthfulness.

This study originated while I was interim pastor of Trinity Mennonite Church in Glendale, Arizona. It was designed to help that congregation get established in Anabaptist-Mennonite theology and practice. Interest in the study was keen, and the congregation profited by finding common ground for faith and practice. In 1985 I used ten chapters of the study in the Lee Heights Community Church in Cleveland, Ohio, an integrated but predominantly black urban congregation. The study was used in a midweek setting, and I used it in preaching on Sundays. In light of the warm response, I am now convinced that the Sermon on the Mount is right at home in the city.

Here are some suggestions for using the book. (1) It can be used as a congregational study. That is what we did in Phoenix. Everyone from MYF age on up used the lessons. On Sundays I preached on the theme that the classes would be discussing. People were encouraged to prepare for Sunday by studying the lessons during the week.

(2) The book can be used as the curriculum for some or all the adult classes without the sermons being geared to the same theme.

(3) Small groups can use it for their study meetings any day of the week.

At the end of each chapter, there are a few pages of blank lines. These are for answering the questions in the sections "Exploring the Text" and "Application to Life." Some adults may feel that writing answers in blank spaces is for children. In this project I have tried to come to grips with the question of what constitutes sound educational methods. There are many ways to learn; and in the best learning environments, many methods are employed. The format of these lessons is designed to reflect a recent development in adult Bible study—inclusion of writing assignments. By including the lesson questions in the discussion, teachers can motivate their classes to take the written answers seriously and do careful preparation.

Regarding the study resources listed in each lesson, I have observed that some people will buy resources if they know which are good books and where they can buy them. The Herald Press books are available at Provident Bookstores. Any of the books can be ordered at a Christian bookstore. The most stimulating book for me was *The Christ of the Mount,* by E. Stanley Jones. He wrote it while serving as a missionary in India. As a result, it has an international perspective appropriate to subject matter that transcends national boundaries.

My prayer for those who use this book is that they will be stimulated to a new love for the Lord and to a new realization that his words on that mountain are the perfect cure for today's moral myopia. Where there is no vision, people perish. The vision is to build a Sermon-on-the-Mount lifestyle. To implement this vision is like building on rock, as in Jesus' parable in the Sermon.

—Jason Martin
Mishawaka, Indiana

References

At the end of each chapter is a section entitled "Additional Study Resources." Most of the references in this section consist of an author and page numbers (for example, Barclay, 78-97). You can find the full reference below by looking under the author. When the reference is to a dictionary or encyclopedia, it will look like this: *Mennonite Encyclopedia*, 'Nonresistance'; or *IDB*, 'Sermon on the Mount.'

Augsburger, David W.
    Caring Enough to Confront. Scottdale, Pa.: Herald Press, 1980.
    Caring Enough to Forgive/Caring Enough Not to Forgive. Scottdale, Pa.: Herald Press, 1981.
    Caring Enough to Hear and Be Heard. Scottdale, Pa.: Herald Press, 1982.
Bair, Ray, and Lillian Bair.
    God's Managers. 2nd edition. Scottdale, Pa.: Herald Press, 1985.
Barclay, William
    The Gospel of Matthew, vol. 1. The Daily Study Bible. Philadelphia: Westminster Press, 1956. (Later editions are available. Page numbers may not correspond to those given in the text.)
Day, Albert
    An Autobiography of Prayer. Nashville: The Upper Room, 1952.

Driver, John
   Kingdom Citizens. Scottdale, Pa.: Herald Press, 1980.
Dyck, Cornelius J.
   Twelve Becoming: Biographies of Mennonite Disciples from the Sixteenth to the Twentieth Century. Newton, Kans.: Faith and Life Press, 1973.
Fairfield, James G. T.
   All That We Are We Give. Scottdale, Pa.: Herald Press, 1977.
Gallardo, Jose
   The Way of Biblical Justice. Mennonite Faith Series, vol. 11. Scottdale, Pa.: Herald Press, 1983.
IDB
   Interpreter's Dictionary of the Bible. 5 vols. Nashville: Abingdon, 1962 (vols. 1-4); 1976 (vol. 5).
Jones, E. Stanley
   The Christ of the Mount. Nashville: Abingdon, 1931. (Later editions are available. Page numbers may not correspond to those given in the text.)
Jordan, Clarence
   The Sermon on the Mount. Valley Forge, Pa.: Judson Press, 1952. (Later edition is available. Page numbers may not correspond to those given in the text.)
Kehler, Larry
   What Mennonites Believe About Money. Scottdale, Pa.: Mennonite Publishing House, 1980.
Kraybill, Ronald S.
   Repairing the Breach: Ministering in Community Conflict. Scottdale, Pa.: Herald Press, 1982.
Lehn, Cornelia
   Peace Be with You. Newton, Kans.: Faith and Life Press, 1980.
Martin, Jason
   The People of God in Community. Scottdale, Pa.: Mennonite Publishing House, 1977.
Mennonite Confession of Faith (1963)
   Scottdale, Pa.: Herald Press, 1963.
The Mennonite Encyclopedia
   4 vols. Mennonite Brethren Publishing House, Mennonite Publication Office (General Conference Mennonite Church), Mennonite Publishing House, 1955-59.
McMillen, S. I.
   None of These Diseases. Old Tappan, N.J.: Fleming H. Revell, 1970.
Miller, John
   The Christian Way. Scottdale, Pa.: Herald Press, 1969.
Richardson, Alan
   A Theological Wordbook of the Bible. New York: Macmillan, 1950.

Rinker, Rosalind
    Prayer: Conversing with God. Grand Rapids, Mich.: Zondervan, 1959.
Sine, Tom
    The Mustard Seed Conspiracy. Waco, Tex.: Word, 1981.
Wenger, J. C.
    Dealing Redemptively with Those Involved in Divorce and Remarriage Problems. Scottdale, Pa.: Herald Press, 1954.
    The Way of Peace. Mennonite Faith Series, vol. 4. Scottdale, Pa.: Herald Press, 1977.
    Mennonite Faith Series, vol. 4. Scottdale, Pa.: Herald Press, 1977.
ZPEB
    Zondervan Pictorial Encyclopedia of the Bible. 5 vols. Grand Rapids, Mich.: Zondervan, 1975.

THE
SERMON
ON THE
MOUNT

*N*OW WHEN HE saw the crowds, he went up on a
mountainside and sat down. His disciples came to him,
and he began to teach them, saying:
> *Blessed are the poor in spirit,*
>> *for theirs is the kingdom of heaven.*
> *Blessed are those who mourn,*
>> *for they will be comforted.*
> *Blessed are the meek,*
>> *for they will inherit the earth.*
> *Blessed are those who hunger and thirst for*
>>> *righteousness,*
>> *for they will be filled.*

Matthew 5:1-6

1

The Beatitudes (I)

SOME PEOPLE'S first move when they begin reading a book is to see how it ends. In this first lesson on the Sermon on the Mount, we may ask how the event ended: "The crowds were amazed at his teaching, because he taught as one who had authority, and not as their teachers of the law" (Matthew 7:28-29). Our initial response to Jesus is to come to terms with his authority, as did the people who first heard the Sermon on the Mount. In light of that, there are three goals for this lesson: (1) to understand the background of the Sermon on the Mount; (2) to see how Matthew draws parallels between Jesus and Moses; (3) to understand the first four beatitudes and apply them to our lives.

Exploring the Text

1. If we fail to see how Matthew built the background for the Sermon on the Mount, we miss something important. Matthew wanted people to see that Jesus was a prophet in the mold of Moses. That may not impress us, but certainly it impressed Matthew. Why was it important to him? Read Matthew 3:13-17. How did Jesus' baptism prepare him for his ministry? What did he receive from John? What did he receive from heaven?

2. Read Matthew 4:1-11. Matthew was eager to show the parallels between Moses and Jesus. Moses spent forty years in the Sinai Desert, where God prepared him for leadership. Jesus spent forty days in the desert deciding what he would and would not do. He was setting goals for his ministry. How did that prepare him for his lifework? Describe the four methods Jesus rejected.

3. In 4:12-17, Matthew quotes from Isaiah 9:1-2. The point is that Jesus is like light overcoming darkness. A basic theme in Jesus' teaching is the coming of the kingdom of God. Did Jesus' call to repentance constitute an invitation to discontinue groping in the dark? What does "the kingdom of God" mean to you? When you pray "Thy kingdom come," what are you requesting?

4. On the shores of Galilee, Jesus found four fishermen. He said to them, "Come, follow me" (4:18-22). Here a new parallel between Moses and Jesus emerges. Read Matthew 4:18-25 and Exodus 3:7-10. Moses was sent by God to bring Israel out of Egyptian darkness. How does Jesus' call to the fishermen and his call to others to repent parallel Moses' work? How is Jesus' liberating work described in Matthew 4:23-25?

5. Large crowds from five regions followed Jesus (4:25). Why were the people attracted to him? Did their interest prepare them to receive Jesus' teaching? If so, how?

6. Read Matthew 5:1-2 (KJV or RSV). When Jesus saw the crowds, he did three things, which have a special underlying significance. What did he do? Which of the three acts reminds you of Moses in Exodus 19:20-22?

7. Read the first four beatitudes with which Jesus began his teaching. What are your impressions of these four sentences? What about them are you unable to understand?

8. Take a look at the grammar used. Are the four sentences imperative (commands) or indicative (describing or reporting)? Can these four virtues be commanded to be in you: poverty of spirit, mourning, meekness, hungering and thirsting for righteousness? Try to write brief definitions for each of these virtues.

The Authority of Jesus

There are people today who are not convinced of Jesus' authority. Some who think he has authority, and would even say so, nevertheless deny it by the way they live. The acid test for acceptance of his authority is not so much what we say about him as what we do about him.

Unbelief is not unique to our age. Probably a larger proportion of the population in Matthew's time than today rejected the idea that Jesus had unique authority. Matthew knew that; and in writing his account of Jesus' life, he organized his material in such a way as to convince as many as possible of Jesus' authority.

The parts of the Gospel of Matthew with which we are particularly concerned are the birth narrative, the accounts of the visit of the magi, the escape from Herod into Egypt, Jesus' baptism and temptation, his proclamation of the kingdom, his calling the disciples, his healing ministry, and the introduction to the Sermon on the Mount in (5:1-2). Matthew carefully arranged these events to convince people that Jesus had the credentials (1) to call people to change their lives, or repent; (2) to ask them to follow him; (3) to liberate them from whatever ailed them; (4) to give them a body of teaching and expect them to live by that teaching.

Bible reading is routinely done in isolated segments. We are often unaware that by doing so we are missing rich meaning. If you begin reading the Sermon on the Mount at 5:1, you might miss the fact that Matthew carefully organized his Gospel to establish a link between Moses and Jesus.

The link between the two was important to Matthew. It is important to us also, but perhaps not for the same reason. We view Moses as a forerunner of, and of lesser importance than, Jesus. For most Jews, Moses was far superior to Jesus. After all, Moses was the great lawgiver; and to suggest that Jesus was like Moses struck these Jews as sacrilegious, to say the least. Matthew wanted to convince people that Jesus was God's anointed one.

What were the parallels between Jesus and Moses? (1) Both were sent from God. (2) Both called people to follow them. (3) Both were liberators. (4) Moses gave a body of teaching, specifically the Ten Commandments, which were to be the pattern for the lifestyle of God's people. Jesus gave the Sermon on the Mount to be the pattern for the lifestyle of his people.

Matthew 5:1-2 includes three somewhat technical phrases that we need to understand: First, "he went up on a mountainside."

Moses had done the same (Exodus 19:20). Moses received the word of God and then gave it to the people. When Jesus went up the mountain, he gave the word of the Lord. He quoted no other authority. What he gave was to be received as authoritative above all other words.

Second, Jesus "sat down." He did the same when he visited the synagogue at Nazareth. After reading Scripture, he sat down to explain it. That was the posture used to give a definitive word in those days—the posture used by teachers in schools and synagogues.

Third, "he opened his mouth" (KJV, RSV, and Greek). Regarding this expression, D. A. Carson says: "We might ask ourselves wryly how he could have taught them without opening his mouth, until we recognize that the expression is a . . . traditional formula. It seems to add deliberateness and sobriety to what follows" (*The Sermon on the Mount* [Grand Rapids, Mich.: Baker Book House, 1978], p. 15). Jesus poured out his heart to the people, giving them what he considered supremely important for their life as the new people of God. There on the mountain Jesus presented the new faith community with a new way to live. The Sermon on the Mount is a brief, authoritative, and life-governing statement from the only one with the authority to make such a statement.

Some people say it is an impossible standard, too high to reach. At first reading it does appear impossible; but the longer you consider it in light of the human situation, the more you are driven to the conclusion that it alone is possible. Everything else is impossible.

The Beatitudes steal up, unobtrusively and quietly, on one who studies them. They are not resounding imperatives, nor do they fit any common human authority structures. They are descriptions of the personality of Jesus' people. As such, they raise eyebrows. After all, don't they dump overboard the success-oriented criteria by which we tend to evaluate people? There is nothing in the Beatitudes that condones our lust for power, greed for money, desire to control destinies, and envy of success. Instead the Beatitudes exalt the poor, the meek, the mourners, and those who hunger and thirst. They are confusing. Superpower statespersons do not speak this language. What is going on in the Beatitudes anyway? Was Jesus talking about otherworldliness, something that has no relevance to real life? Not at all. Jesus was opening a window on what is wrong with the value system that we take for granted but that Jesus could never accept. Those who are liberated from the enslaving world-system, Jesus said, have characters that reflect the Beatitudes. I like what William Barclay says:

> The blessedness which belongs to the Christian is not a blessedness which is postponed to some future world of glory; it is a blessedness which exists here and now. . . . The Beatitudes in effect say, "O the sheer happiness of knowing Jesus Christ as Master, Savior and Lord!. . ." In face of the Beatitudes, a gloom-encompassed Christianity is unthinkable (*The Gospel of Matthew,* vol. 1, pp. 83-84).

Jesus described a blessedness for here and now. That means it should be practical. In thinking about how this lesson can be practical, consider the contrast between human aggressiveness and the character described in the first three beatitudes. Hostility and aggression are tremendous forces in life. In Jesus' description of his disciples there is a force that is altogether different.

> The first three Beatitudes . . . show God's invasion of us, taking away our self-sufficiency, our very self-life, getting us ready for the most amazing offensive of love the world has ever seen. He disarms us in order to put entirely new weapons into our hands. Unless these three verses become actual the rest of the Sermon on the Mount becomes impossible. The rub is at the place of letting go of the essential self. Do that and turning the other cheek is a necessary and natural outcome.
> To sum up: the renounced in spirit gain the kingdom of heaven; the mourners gain the kingdom of inner comfort; the meek gain the earth. So the world above, the world within, and the world around belong to this person. Wanting nothing, she or he inherits all worlds (E. Stanley Jones, *The Christ of the Mount,* p. 71).

Application to Life

1. This lesson is studded with references to Jesus' authority. It is easier to speak theoretically about that than practically. Were there new perceptions of his authority for you? Authority is made practical by obedience. In that case, where do you accept Jesus' authority? Where do you reject it? What changes would you like to see in yourself?

2. What is your emotional response to the first four beatitudes? What is your rational response? Do these beatitudes describe you? E. Stanley Jones says that Jesus "disarms us in order to put entirely new weapons into our hands." What weapons would they be?

Additional Study Resources

Barclay, 78-97; Driver, 55-66; Jones 49-70; Jordan, 9-26; *IDB* and *ZPEB*, 'Sermon on the Mount' and 'Beatitudes'.

Notes

BLESSED ARE the merciful,
　　for they will be shown mercy.
Blessed are the pure in heart,
　　for they will see God.
Blessed are the peacemakers,
　　for they will be called sons of God.
Blessed are those who are persecuted because of
　　　　righteousness,
　　for theirs is the kingdom of heaven.
*Blessed are you when people insult you, persecute you
and falsely say all kinds of evil against you because of
me. Rejoice and be glad, because great is your reward in
heaven, for in the same way they persecuted the prophets
who were before you.*

Matthew 5:7-12

2

The Beatitudes (II)

EXAMINATIONS are inevitable for students. An exam determines whether the students have learned the subject matter. If not, they receive a failing grade. When we have health problems, we see a doctor; and he or she examines us to find out what the problem is and how to treat it. Examinations that give bad news cause pain.

The Beatitudes are an examination too. In them we face self-examination. That may be the most painful kind of all. The Beatitudes are Jesus' description of his disciples. In our lesson text, Jesus says, "Blessed are you—the merciful, the pure in heart, the peacemakers, and the persecuted." The disciple's first response is, "I am?" The second is, "Am I?" When we learn what Jesus is making of us, we are first surprised and then dismayed. The purpose of this lesson is self-examination by asking: (1) How did Jesus describe his people? (2) How do I measure up?

Exploring the Text

1. The character of Christians as Jesus visualized it is described in the Beatitudes. Some people say that the Beatitudes were only an ideal he taught, that they do not have relevance for the realities

people face in life. Do you think of them as only an ideal he taught, or was Jesus that kind of man? Are you that kind of person?

2. Self-examination that has integrity is difficult. Self- examination often lacks integrity for two reasons. One, we routinely distort the truth to make it personally acceptable; and, two, we do not use a reliable, objective standard to guide us. The Beatitudes are such a standard. Some people have found a support group indispensable to give self-examination more integrity. In a spirit of self-examination, ask yourself:

a. Regarding mercy—do I forgive those who wrong me in the way Jesus teaches us to forgive in Matthew 18:15-17?

b. Regarding purity—are my motives pure, or are they mixed? (See James 4:8.)

c. Regarding peacemaking—in situations where I am involved, are people more sensitive and loving because of me? Or do I cause tension, hostility, and problems?

d. Regarding persecution—do I have the backbone to stand up for the right even when I have to make a personal sacrifice?

3. Write your definition of the following: *merciful, pure in heart, peacemakers, persecuted.* Perhaps it would be helpful to think of persons who have demonstrated these qualities. What did they do that characterized them as the following?

4. Do you think the Beatitudes should be viewed as describing all the members of the body of Christ?

5. Jesus said that his disciples *are* merciful, pure in heart, peacemakers, and persecuted. How do they become such people? Read Romans 8:1-2 and 2 Corinthians 5:17.

6. What response will you receive in the world if your character and conduct are what Jesus said they will be?

The Scars of Conflict

The apostle Thomas was not easily convinced of Jesus' resurrection. He said, "Unless I see the nail marks in his hands and put my fingers where the nails were, and put my hand into his side, I will not believe it" (John 20:25). One week later Jesus came to Thomas and asked him to touch the places where the nails and the spear had pierced him. Jesus bore scars of conflict. When Thomas saw them, he was convinced.

Jesus apparently knew that people with the character of the Beatitudes will also bear scars of conflict. The progression in the Beatitudes leads to persecution, from which Jesus' followers receive scars. There always are skeptics who are convinced only by these scars.

No one wants wounds that lead to being scarred. Perhaps that is why the Sermon on the Mount has often been regarded as too idealistic for everyday living. It is sad that the Sermon has often been made a marginal set of teaching by the very church that is to be motivated and shaped by that teaching.

From the second to the fifth centuries the church developed a number of creeds that effectively displaced the Sermon on the Mount from its earlier central place as a pattern for the lifestyle of Christians. The creeds were statements of belief formulated by human logic. It was assumed that if people believed in the correctly formulated creed, they were Christian.

One person who was included as a Christian was Constantine, the Roman emperor who died in A.D. 337. His life and practice was only remotely like the description in the Sermon on the Mount; yet the church, with its emphasis on doctrine and neglect of practice, rushed to accept Constantine. In fact he presided at the Council of Nicaea (A.D. 325), which convened to form a creed. (This creed is included in *The Mennonite Hymnal* as an affirmation of faith.) Constantine was even called "bishop of bishops" although he still lived like a pagan warrior and was not baptized until near death twelve years later. He could recite the creeds but did not have the deeds. One wonders how church history might have been different if recitation of the creeds had been followed with recitation of the Sermon on the Mount. A church that lived by the Sermon would not have been conquered by a pagan warrior.

The first Christians were called, not to a creedal faith, but to the simple confession that "Jesus is Lord" (Romans 10:9; 1 Corinthians 12:3). Once that confession was made, then the believer was taught how to live as a Christian. The basic guide was the Sermon on the Mount. Creedal faith still dominates the Christian church far too much. John Miller describes the outcome: "As a result, Jesus himself is deprived of any significant authority in the Church as a spokesman for His own movement" (*The Christian Way,* p. 4).

Jesus' movement is the kingdom of God.

Life in the natural order is often characterized by hostility, aggression, pride, and self-centeredness. The new order of Jesus Christ, which he called "the kingdom of God," stands in vivid contrast to the world order. This new order is characterized by poverty of spirit, sadness about sin, and meekness. When Jesus began to preach, "Repent, for the kingdom of heaven is near," he was inviting people to leave the bondage of the world order and be liberated into God's intended order, to become what they were created to be. The appeal of the gospel is to be what you were meant to be. Nothing else will satisfy the human heart.

Some people view the character of the kingdom as expressed in the Beatitudes as weakness. Are not poverty, mourning, and meekness signs of weakness? National leaders seem to think so. A series of U.S. leaders have said repeatedly that the only way to negotiate with the enemy is to be militarily stronger than the enemy. Television programming models the same principle for personal life.

Our culture is saturated with hostility and aggression. This is the setting in which we are to be faithful to Jesus' kingdom teaching. What are his people like? What does it mean to be what you are meant to be? The answer is found in the Sermon on the Mount in two forms: (1) the description of the believer's character in the Beatitudes, and (2) the description of the believer's practice in the rest of the Sermon.

In real life it is assumed that power meets power and the spoils go to the person at the top. Those who think that the kingdom-of-God character is too weak to face real life should think carefully about what it was that Jesus actually taught. It may appear that to be persecuted is to be passive, but that is a superficial reading. There is nothing cowardly about it; nor did Jesus counsel a passive, serene withdrawal from the bruising, bloody battle. He said that we are to be peacemakers; and, as I see it, that takes toughness, courage, and wisdom that only God can give. We need to be rooted into the ground of our being.

Jesus was a peacemaker. He did it in hand-to-hand combat with evil. There was no passive withdrawal. When Thomas wanted to see Jesus' credentials, Jesus offered the scars of conflict, and the scars convinced him. Today, people who are terrorized by a sense of standing on the brink of nuclear disaster need to see the scars of peacemakers at work. The nuclear threat is an international crisis. If you feel you cannot tackle a problem so immense, remember that there is no lack of need for personalized, close-to-home peacemaking.

Application to Life

1. The focus of this lesson is the kind of followers Jesus wants in a world that is saturated with hostility, aggressiveness, and violence that needs peacemakers. What situations have you seen, heard of, or been involved in where you saw the need for peacemakers? Could you have been one then, or were gifts other than yours required?

2. Nuclear-age realities and those of A.D. 30 seem so dissimilar that one wonders whether a teaching given back then can be relevant today. How can you personally fill your role as peacemaker? What could your congregation do? In peacemaking, what actions have you taken or seen that you are proud of?

3. Jot down one or more things that you would like to see happen in your family or community that would make for peace.

Additional Study Resources

Barclay, 97-114; Driver, 66-72; Jones 72-85; Jordan, 27-44; *IDB* and *ZPEB,* 'Sermon on the Mount' and 'Beatitudes'.

Notes

_____

_____

_____

_____

_____

_____

_____

_____

_____

YOU ARE THE SALT of the earth. But if the salt loses its saltiness, how can it be made salty again? It is no longer good for anything, except to be thrown out and trampled by men.

You are the light of the world. A city on a hill cannot be hidden. Neither do people light a lamp and put it under a bowl. Instead they put it on its stand, and it gives light to everyone in the house. In the same way, let your light shine before men, that they may see your good deeds and praise your Father in heaven.

Matthew 5:13-16

3

*Christians
and the World*

PREMIUM-GRADE discipleship teaching—that is the essence of
the Sermon on the Mount. It was given to shape the lifestyle of
Jesus' people. In the first centuries after Christ, the church used the
Sermon to instruct new believers about how to live as Christians. In
the Anabaptist-Mennonite spiritual stream, the Sermon was given
the same priority. Although it may not have been formal instruc-
tional material for new believers, it certainly was the life guide for
all believers. Used in that way, it is still as vital to believers as it ever
was. In this lesson we face this question of discipleship: What is it
that makes disciples salt to the earth and light to the world?

Exploring the Text
1. In biblical times salt had two well-known domestic uses: to
preserve some foods and to add flavor to food. Salt also is essential
for health. In Leviticus 2:13 it is included as a mandatory part of of-
ferings. What are the qualities of salt that led Jesus to describe his
people as "the salt of the earth"?

2. If Christians prevent spoilage, how do they do it? In what
ways does faith add sparkle and flavor to life? Is your life a joy or a
drag?

3. Salt is used in a metaphorical sense elsewhere in the Bible. In Deuteronomy 29:23 and Zephaniah 2:9 barren heaps of salt represent the barrenness and sterility of unbelief. That metaphor brings to mind the imagery in Jesus' teaching: "But if the salt loses its saltiness, how can it be made salty again?" What answer would you give to Jesus' question? What answer do you think he expected? Was it a rhetorical question, which did not need an answer? If the question was rhetorical, what point was Jesus trying to make?

4. "You are the salt of the earth"—this is not a command; it is a statement of fact. The form of speech Jesus used gives the same impression as that conveyed in the Beatitudes. Jesus was telling his people what they already were. The statement is highly positive. Reflect on its meaning for you. How would you feel if Jesus stood face-to-face with you and said, "You are the salt of the earth"? Or would you rather hear it this way: "Go and work hard at being salt"?

5. Read Mark 9:49-50. Verse 49 refers to the purifying quality of salt. Think carefully about the following statement from verse 50: "Have salt in yourselves." How does it differ from the statement "You are the salt"? How do you think people can have salt in themselves?

6. 'You are the light of the world.... Let your light shine before men." The first statement is indicative, *describing* the disciples. The second is imperative, *commanding* them to shine. What other Bible verses do you know that help you understand the meaning of being the light of the world? See John 8:12; 9:5; 1 Peter 2:9-12. What is the difference between the benefits that salt and light provide?

7. Jesus pointed out that there is a purpose for letting our light shine: "that they may see your good deeds and praise your Father in heaven." The matter of discipleship comes clearly to the forefront here. What is discipleship? Why do good deeds lead people to praise God?

Saltless Salt

E. Stanley Jones wrote *The Christ of the Mount* in 1931 while a missionary in India. In that book he presents the Beatitudes as Jesus' statement of what Christians are to themselves. However, he notes that when Jesus told the disciples they were salt and light, he shifted the focus away from what Christians are to themselves to what they are to the world.

Jesus' statements "You are the salt of the earth" and "You are the light of the world" certainly address an issue that permanently confronts the church: What is the church's relationship to the world? There are perhaps two ways to look at it. One is attitudinal—how we *think* about our place in the world. The other is functional—what we are to *do* in the world. Salt and light as spoken about by Jesus define function.

There have been different perspectives of how the church is to relate to the world. Every disciple of Jesus has a view on the issue. There is no way to avoid it. Jesus and the apostles saw it as a matter of the believers being called out of the world to be a redeemed people, who were then to turn back to the world, taking to it the redeeming gospel of Jesus Christ. That view rested on the understanding that humanity is lost and there is no solution for its lostness short of being liberated from the world—leaving behind all old loyalties in favor of new loyalties to Jesus as Lord and to the church, the community of faith.

In the fourth century, the church-world relationship was reformulated. The church had so effectively evangelized the world that people began to think of the world as Christian. When Emperor Constantine granted the church official toleration and apparently became a Christian himself, the church and world closed ranks and said, "We are one." And why not since even the emperor was a believer?

However, the vital issue had simply been overlooked. Constantine's unchristian conduct was ignored. After his supposed conversion, Constantine murdered his brother-in-law; sentenced his eleven-year-old nephew to die; killed his oldest son, Crispus; arranged the death of his second wife; and used nails that allegedly came from Christ's cross in his war helmet and on the bridle of his war-horse. Constantine may have professed faith, but it was without discipleship. He did not let his good deeds "shine before men."

In the reformulation of the church-world issue in the fourth century, the church had become worldly rather than the world becoming like the church. Its focal point was a far cry from the cross on Calvary and the Sermon on the Mount. The fourth-century concept of a Christianized world continued to dominate the church's thinking and practice until the Protestant Reformation. Even then, only the Anabaptists were ready to dump Constantinianism and attempt a radical return to Christ's and the apostles' view of the relationship between the church and the world.

The lesson one might draw from church history is that the requirements of Sermon-on-the-Mount discipleship are heavy, and the church failed to live up to the Sermon because it is impossible to do so. Or is the Sermon as a guide for life outmoded? That would be a hard pill to swallow, because it suggests that Constantine was on the right track after all. It also would mean that he, not Jesus, had the best solution for Christians as they try to relate to the world.

There is no question about the difficulty involved in living by the Sermon on the Mount. Church history verifies that. But it does not verify that the Sermon is outmoded. All that is verifiable is that it is Jesus' word for his people—his sense-making, wholeness-producing word even for twentieth-century Christians. If this present world is going to praise God because of our good deeds, it will be because people live by the Sermon on the Mount.

We receive the same surprising word that Jesus' fishermen-disciples heard. They were the hope of the world. They were to end life's banality by injecting life with zest. They were to end the rottenness by making society sound. They were to provide light, penetrating the darkness so that people could see.

It was a surprising word because of the people it was given to. They may have been the most improbable world-changers ever assembled. Jesus turned the task over to them, and they made a notable difference in the world.

After Jesus had given his astonishing assessment of the disciples, he offered a warning: the disciples could "blow" the world vision either by losing their saltiness or by hiding their light. I like both the assessment and the warning. They underscore the significance of human life. We are the world's hope; and if we fail, the hope is lost. Jesus attached great value to our lives. Our discipleship is for the healing of the world. Many people struggle with a lack of purpose. Jesus' vision would heal them. No disciple of Jesus should feel useless, not with the importance Jesus gave to discipleship.

There is at present a renewed awareness in the church in many parts of the world that people need a close support group to help them be faithful disciples. That is encouraging, for it is very difficult to be a disciple without strong support.

Application to Life

1. What would you like to see happen in your congregation that would make it more attractive to unchurched people? Is working at improving congregational life one of the ways to be salty?

2. Oliver Wendell Holmes once said, "I might have entered the ministry if clergymen I knew had not looked and acted so much like undertakers." Does saltiness cause solemnity or does it put smiles on faces?

3. Being the light of the world is a matter of letting people see our good deeds. What does that involve—a life of discipleship or something else? In light of this lesson, what is your commitment to action?

Additional Study Resources

Barclay, 114-22; Driver, 72-74; Jones, 86-99; Jordan, 36-44; Miller, 36-38; *IDB* and *ZPEB*, 'Salt' and 'Light'.

Notes

_____

_____

_____

_____

_____

_____

_____

_____

_____

Do NOT THINK that I have come to abolish the Law or the Prophets; I have not come to abolish them but to fulfill them. I tell you the truth, until heaven and earth disappear, not the smallest letter, not the least stroke of a pen, will by any means disappear from the Law until everything is accomplished. Anyone who breaks one of the least of these commandments and teaches others to do the same will be called least in the kingdom of heaven, but whoever practices and teaches these commands will be called great in the kingdom of heaven. For I tell you that unless your righteousness surpasses that of the Pharisees and the teachers of the law, you will certainly not enter the kingdom of heaven.

Matthew 5:17-20

4

*Jesus
and the Law*

"WE COME NOW to one of the most important statements that ever fell from the lips of Jesus." That is E. Stanley Jones' evaluation of Matthew 5:17-20. And William Barclay says this about the passage in his commentary: "At first reading it might well be held that this is the most astonishing statement that Jesus made in the whole Sermon on the Mount."

Most astonishing, most important—the statement may be neither of those, but Jesus' relationship to the Law was continually on people's minds, as the Gospels reveal. That issue finally led to his death on the cross when his enemies charged that he had undermined their national religion. It is important for us to understand how Jesus viewed himself in relation to the Law.

Exploring the Text

1. Jesus came, not to abolish, but to fulfill the Law and the Prophets. How did he fulfill them? Is he still fulfilling them?

2. In Romans 10:4 Paul says, "Christ is the end of the law." In what way is this true?

3. The Law has a permanence exceeding that of the universe. What is the source of the Law's dynamic? See Jeremiah 1:12.

4. Failure to practice and teach even the least important commandments has a bad consequence. What is it?

5. What is the result of practicing and teaching the least important commandments? What does it mean to be great in the kingdom?

6. The Law included moral and ethical guidelines for God's people. Do we need such guidelines? If so, what benefit do they provide?

7. What understanding of human nature is assumed in verse 19?

8. Verse 20 is a sharp indictment of the Pharisees and teachers of the Law. How was their righteousness deficient?

9. We need to look at the New Testament definition of righteousness. How is righteousness defined in (a) Mark 12:28-34; (b) Romans 13:8-10; (c) Romans 1:16-17; 3:21-26; (d) James 2:8?

10. What conclusions do you arrive at from Matthew 5:17-20 and the verses listed in question 9?

Righteousness—Achieved or Received?

Righteousness, at least in humans, consists of two things. First, it is to be in right relationship with God; second, it is to live a good life. The first kind of righteousness is received, not achieved. The second kind is achieved, not received—at least it is more achieved and less received than the first kind.

God gave us an offer of right relationship with him through Jesus Christ. We receive it by faith. It is a gift that cannot be earned. God also invites us to live righteously; and because it is something we can work at, righteous living seems to be achievable. In fact, however, it too is received, for God gives both ethical rules and the power to keep them. We are far more dependent on God's grace than we are usually aware.

What is the way to God?—that is the implicit question in the preceding paragraphs. It is also the issue in Jesus' teaching in Matthew 5:17-20. The issue is focused most clearly in verse 20, in the incisive critique of the deficient righteousness of the Pharisees and the teachers of the Law.

These men were in the business of earning their salvation by keeping the law. They were legalists. If they did more right than wrong, they believed, then God would accept them and they would be righteous.

Jesus emphatically rejected their works-righteousness. Unless people's righteousness exceeds righteousness based on works, they will not make it into God's kingdom. In other words, righteousness cannot be achieved through human effort. It can only be received by faith.

Some people are attracted to the notion that keeping the rules is the way to find God. Jesus found that notion present in his time and rejected it. There were four misguided approaches to the Law that Jesus responded to.

1. Some people viewed the Law as a mediator. They believed that by keeping the rules they could find and please God. Jesus severely criticized and rejected that thinking. That is the point of his parables in Luke 15.

2. Jesus rejected externalization of the Law. Mere outward conformity is not acceptable. The inner person must be captivated by and tuned in to God. Jesus said that the greatest commandment is to love God totally—with heart, soul, and strength (compare Deuteronomy 6:5 and Matthew 22:34-40).

3. Jesus rejected using the Law to protect a person's disobedience to God. See Matthew 15:1-6 for an example of such use of the Law. Another example is found in 5:31-32. People vigorously condemned adultery as a violation of the Law, but then they used another part of the Law to allow easy divorce so that they could commit adultery anyway.

4. Jesus rejected using the Law to gain personal recognition (Matthew 6:1-18).

A pertinent question is, What difference does Jesus' teaching about the Law make to us? In 1982-83 I was interim pastor of Trinity Mennonite Church in Glendale, Arizona. During part of that time, I directed the congregation in a study of the Sermon on the Mount. Norma Godshall led a women's Bible study. The group was using these lessons, so I asked her how she planned to teach regarding Jesus and the Law. She responded, "When I think about what Jesus said, it seems unfair. He said he did not come to abolish the rules. That means they're still there facing me, for me to keep, and I can't keep them. That's unfair. There they are. I've violated them and my mistakes seem unforgivable. It's like playing a game where you feel you can't win. But there is a way to win—Jesus Christ."

Norma's predicament is universal. No one can keep the rules—at least not well enough to earn God's love. Norma's solution—Jesus Christ—is also for everyone.

The biblical view of rules for God's people is that they are the way we respond to God's love, not the way we earn it. A clear example of that viewpoint is found in Romans 12:1: "Therefore, I urge you, brothers, *in view of God's mercy*, to offer your bodies as living sacrifices, holy and pleasing to God—which is your spiritual worship. The point of the sentence is that offering ourselves in a holy lifestyle is *our appropriate response to God's mercy.* God's mercy was demonstrated in Jesus Christ.

This verse also marks a shift in the epistle as a whole. Romans 1-11 is a proclamation of God's mercy through Jesus Christ. It is the gospel of Jesus Christ according to Paul. Romans 12-15 provides rules for living a holy life. Following them is viewed as the believer's response to having received salvation through Christ. The Letter to the Romans shows the relationship between God's grace and rules in the New Testament. Righteousness as having a *right relationship with God* is a *gift* of his grace. Righteousness as living a *holy life* is a *response* to God's grace.

Is the Old Testament approach different from that of the New Testament? I think not. Sometimes the word *Law* in the New Testament means the Ten Commandments. The Hebrews called them the Ten Words. And these Ten Words are crucial in understanding the way to God in the Old Testament. The Ten Words are found in Exodus 20:1-17, but all Christian listings of the Ten Commandments include only verses 3-17. That is a serious flaw, simply because it omits the word of grace: "I am the Lord your God, who brought you out of Egypt, out of the land of slavery." Jewish listings of the Ten Words always include the word of grace. Any recitation of the Ten Commandments that omits the word of grace is nonsense—and even worse—for it seriously blinds people to the biblical view of grace and law.

The Hebrew word for the Law is *Torah*. In the Old Testament the priority is always grace and then Torah. Grace was first, and living by the Torah was the people's response to grace. The heartbeat of Scripture is that grace always precedes law. Following the law is the people's response to grace. The organization of Romans into sections on grace (chapters 1-11) and law (chapters 12-15) is like the organization of the first five books of the Bible. Genesis and Exodus 1—20:2 describe God's saving work. Exodus 20:3 through Deuteronomy describes how the people are to respond to God's grace.

What is Jesus' relationship to the Law? Precisely that the grace-Torah heartbeat is more enduring than planet Earth. Furthermore, Jesus himself is grace, and all who turn to him can then live for him by his rules. That reality has clear implications for interpreting the Sermon on the Mount. Matthew 5:3-16—the Beatitudes and the salt-light passage—describes the transformed character of people saved by God's grace. Matthew 5:17—7:27 describes how people are to live in response to God's saving grace.

Application to Life

1. What conclusions have you arrived at in your study of Jesus and the Law?

2. Can anyone be faithful to Christ without a Sermon-on-the-Mount lifestyle?

Additional Study Resources

Barclay, 122-28; Driver, 74-78; Jones, 100-128; Jordan, 45-53; Miller, 40-45; *IDB,* 'Canon'; *ZPEB,* 'Canon', 'Law', and 'Nature of Man'.

Notes

_____

_____

_____

_____

_____

_____

_____

YOU HAVE HEARD that it was said to the people long ago, "Do not murder, and anyone who murders will be subject to judgment." But I tell you that anyone who is angry with his brother will be subject to judgment. Again, anyone who says to his brother, "Raca," is answerable to the Sanhedrin. But anyone who says, "You fool!" will be in danger of the fire of hell.

Therefore, if you are offering your gift at the altar and there remember that your brother has something against you, leave your gift there in front of the altar. First go and be reconciled to your brother; then come and offer your gift.

Settle matters quickly with your adversary who is taking you to court. Do it while you are still with him on the way, or he may hand you over to the judge, and the judge may hand you over to the officer, and you may be thrown into prison. I tell you the truth, you will not get out until you have paid the last penny.

Matthew 5:21-26

5

---

*Anger
and Conflict
Resolution*

ANGER CAN be regarded as a negative emotion, sure to cause
trouble if it isn't carefully controlled. It can also be viewed posi-
tively, as helpful if rightly used. It is hardly ever viewed neutrally, as
though it didn't matter. Thomas Jefferson's advice "When angry,
count ten before you speak; if very angry, an hundred" sounds like
that of James: "Everyone should be quick to listen, slow to speak
and slow to become angry, for man's anger does not bring about
the righteous life that God desires" (1:19). The focus of this chapter
is everyone's concern—what to do with anger.

Exploring the Text

1. In the Sermon on the Mount, Jesus drew a contrast between
what "was said to the people long ago" and what he wanted them
to hear (Matthew 5:21-22). How would you describe the contrast?

2. Jesus described three negative responses to another person.
What is the destination of (a) one who is angry; (b) one who says,
"Raca"; (c) one who says, "You fool!" What does it mean (a) to be
angry; (b) to say, "Raca"; (c) to say, "You fool!"?

Do the three responses belong together in one outburst of
emotion, or are they to be seen as isolated? If they belong together,

are they progressive? That is, is saying "Raca" worse than anger; and saying "You fool!" worse than saying "Raca"? Are all three responses an expression of anger?

3. Jesus uses the word *brother* four times in verses 21-26. What does that suggest as to the setting where Jesus' teaching will be heard and practiced?

4. *Therefore* is used as a linking word between verses 22 and 23. Why is it there? Is there an obvious connection? What is the problem in this passage?

5. Jesus appears to address a similar problem in Matthew 18:15-20 and Matthew 5:23-24. What is alike in the two passages? What is different? In Matthew 18:21-35 there is a parable about forgiveness. What light does the parable shed on Matthew 18:15-20?

6. In Matthew 5:25-26 the problem is a disagreement in which one party is being taken to court by an adversary. What solution did Jesus recommend? Why is it better to settle matters while still on the way to court? Is there something bad about court settlements? If so, what?

7. Read Paul's continuation of Jesus' teaching about believers and lawsuits in 1 Corinthians 6:1-11. Did Paul approve of Christians going to court? Who did Paul think should settle disputes? In light of Jesus' and Paul's words about settling matters out of court, what do you think was accepted New Testament practice?

8. There was also follow-up teaching about anger by the apostles. Read Ephesians 4:26-27 and James 1:19-20. In what ways did Paul and James support Jesus' teaching?

Anger—the Fiery Emotion

Since anger is so often maligned, we are likely to forget that it is a God-given emotion just as others are. Normal people laugh, cry, love, and become angry. In the right doses at the right times for the right reasons, anger can bring about the right results. Misused, it brings the wrong results. An angry outburst can strain a friendship for years and often ends it outright.

Jesus became angry. He was apparently not afraid of it in himself or in others. He accepted it as a human capability that, like others, needs to be controlled. One Sabbath, a man with a shriveled hand was present in a synagogue. Some people were there to see whether Jesus would heal the man, whether he would violate their rule that healing on the Sabbath was acceptable only to save a life. In this situation, Jesus "looked around at them in anger" (Mark 3:5). Then Jesus healed the man. It was a gripping moment when Jesus' anger highlighted the colossal idiocy of considering a trivial Sabbath rule of greater value than a person in need.

Jesus' anger was aroused by injustice—a good reason to be angry. Too often we become unjustifiably angry when our demands are not met. Unless our demands concern a genuine justice issue, we have become angry for wrong reasons. Anger for such reasons requires confession, a forthright admission—"I am angry."

The Bible provides many interesting insights into conflict and attempts to resolve it. Sin appears to be the root of conflict; for as soon as Eve and Adam sinned, it began. It is helpful to see how the first chapters of the Bible link conflict with sin and how some people there responded to conflict.

Adam and Eve tried to pass the buck. Adam said, "The woman you put here with me—she gave me some fruit from the tree, and I ate it" (Genesis 3:12). Eve responded, "The serpent deceived me, and I ate" (verse 13).

Cain killed Abel to handle their conflict. Cain was very angry. He killed Abel. His solution was unsatisfactory and he finally said, "My punishment is more than I can bear" (Genesis 4:13).

Lamech believed in unlimited retaliation. He said to his wives, "I have killed a man for wounding me, a young man for injuring me. If Cain is avenged seven times, then Lamech seventy-seven times" (Genesis 4:23-24).

Conflict exists wherever there are people. Conflict leads to anger. The goal is not to attempt an unrealistic effort to eliminate all conflict. The issue is how to resolve conflict when it arises and how to handle our angry feelings in conflict situations.

Jesus was not one to duck issues. He dealt with our conflicts and our anger in the Sermon on the Mount. He gave us instructions regarding what to do in conflict and how to handle our anger. He spoke as one with authority, contrasting what "was said to the people long ago" with his own teaching—"But I tell you. . . ."

Jesus' word about anger and conflict makes sense for our time. Much that has been written and spoken in the twentieth century does not. I am impressed that Jesus' teaching, if followed, will heal our anger in the church and help us to resolve our conflicts and to be a light to the world.

Some people today, like some in Jesus' time, think that murder is wrong but anger is harmless. Jesus held to the murder-is-wrong view, of course, but rejected the notion that anger is harmless. There is a widespread view of anger called the ventilation theory. It holds that the way to deal with our anger is to "blow off steam." After doing so, one will presumably feel better. This theory views us as though we were steel water tanks with a fire underneath. Blowing off now and then supposedly is going to keep the pressure at safe levels.

The truth about us is that we are not like pressure tanks, and ventilating anger is only helpful sometimes. More often, ventilating anger actually delays getting over it. Frequently, angry outbursts make resolution more difficult. In a book by Carol Tavris, *Anger: The Misunderstood Emotion* (Simon and Schuster, 1982), the author draws on numerous studies of anger that show the best way to handle angry feelings is not to "pop off" but to control them. The effect of the ventilation theory has been to cause more noise in our lives but not to lessen our problems. It is, after all, as our mothers taught us—we should control our anger; we should cool off before popping off. Giving vent to anger is a threat to friendships, and friendships have more value than a momentary need to tell off a person. People who give vent to their rage become more rather than less angry. The shortest route to getting over anger is to control it.

If ventilating is the wrong approach, what is more helpful? Here are some principles that are based on Jesus' and the apostles' teachings and that agree with the best of modern studies.

One, anger is always serious. Do not regard it lightly (but a sense of humor is useful in healing anger). Two, when you are angry or have hurt feelings, be ready to enter into dialogue before the sun goes down. Three, it is useless just to talk about the anger. It is helpful to know that anger is loaded with demands. Since anger is not negotiable and demands are, get behind the anger to the demands. Then you can settle matters.

The demands are often hidden, like seven eighths of an iceberg; only the anger, one eighth of the iceberg, shows. When an ocean vessel hits an iceberg, it is not the tip that rips the ship. So also with anger. It's the hidden demands that you have to watch out for: "Do not criticize me"; "Don't interfere with my program"; "Do not reject me"; "Don't take advantage of me"; "Do not make me fail."

Such demands are unrealistic and destructive. However, there are fair demands: "I want an equal hearing with you"; "Regard me as trustworthy"; "I demand a regard for myself equal to that for others."

To conclude, on page 64 is a summary of ways in which people try to resolve conflict. The ideal is collaboration—the point where persons are in touch with their feelings and are willing and able to speak honestly with each other.

Application to Life

1. Conflict is often difficult to handle. What is the most recent conflict situation you have been involved in that made you feel helpless? What is your concept of Jesus' way to work at conflict?

2. Lawsuits have a pervasive hold on people's lives. Some doctors pay as much as $80,000 annually for malpractice insurance. Can Jesus' disciples participate in the lawsuit industry? What do court settlements mean for litigants' emotions? Efforts such as VORP—Victim Offender Reconciliation Program—which began in northern Indiana, bring criminals and their victims together and try to find court-approved resolution of crimes. Could your congregation support such a program?

3. Anger usually goes with conflict. What have you found to be the best way for you to resolve angry feelings? Can you resolve them before the sun sets? What help would you like to see from your congregation to enable you and others to deal with anger?

Additional Study Resources

Augsburger, *Caring Enough to Confront; Caring Enough to Forgive/ Not Forgive;* Barclay, 134-43; Driver, 80-84; Jones, 131-44; Jordan, 54-62; Kraybill, *Repairing the Breach*; Martin, 93-98; Miller, 47-50; *IDB* and *ZPEB*, 'Anger' and 'Sermon on the Mount'.

Five Styles of Conflict Resolution

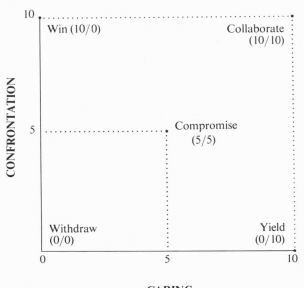

CARING

Withdraw (0/0): For various reasons, persons may choose to avoid conflict altogether by refusing to confront the issues either by denying their existence or simply ignoring them.

Win (10/0): One person has a clear need to be *the* winner. Blaming, cajoling, harassment, and seeking revenge may be aspects of the relationship.

Yield (0/10): The essence of this style is accommodation—giving in. This may be an expression of genuine caring, or it may be a mode of copping out, because it is easier than confronting the issues head on.

Compromise (5/5): Here the key is conceding. Each person gives a little to gain a little. Neither party is satisfied fully, but the result is better than both parties being completely unsatisfied.

Collaborate (10/10): In this strategy, both sides are satisfied, both sides win. There are very few times when persons actually reach this point. The real value is that both are willing to make their feelings known and then work toward a reasonable solution. This requires that both parties be flexible. In healthy caring-confrontation, growth and change are going to happen.

Source: Address by Jep and Joyce Hostetler to the Mennonite Health Association, 13 March 1982, Louisville, Kentucky.

Notes

YOU HAVE HEARD that it was said, "Do not commit adultery." But I tell you that anyone who looks at a woman lustfully has already committed adultery with her in his heart. If your right eye causes you to sin, gouge it out and throw it away. It is better for you to lose one part of your body than for your whole body to be thrown into hell. And if your right hand causes you to sin, cut it off and throw it away. It is better for you to lose one part of your body than for your whole body to go into hell.

Matthew 5:27-30

6

Sexuality

THE WORD *sexuality* is gaining currency; and I, for one, am pleased about it. *Sexuality* avoids the narrower definition of the word *sex,* as well as its gutter connotations. *Sex* often is simply a synonym for intercourse, which according to Jesus' teaching can be pure and admirable. But in our cultural setting, it is hard to rescue the word *sex* from its negative connotations.

Sexuality is a more inclusive term, referring to all that is involved in being created female or male. Sexuality refers to the condition of being either male or female with all its spiritual, physical, emotional, social, economic, religious, and political implications.

Since there is no possibility of covering all of this in one session, the focus of this lesson is to try to learn what are the principles of sexuality taught by Jesus. We need to know how to cope with our sexuality maturely, not allowing it to become destructive.

Exploring the Text

1. In Matthew 5:27-28 two aspects of sexuality are brought into focus: an act and an attitude. The two aspects are distinguished in two of the Ten Commandments—Exodus 20:14, 17. What is the act? What is the attitude?

2. In our text Jesus draws a contrast, for the second time, using the following expression: "You have heard that it was said. . . . But I tell you. . . ." What do you think Jesus meant to convey by this contrast? What is the difference between what the people had heard before and what they now heard from Jesus? What kind of sexual conduct do you think Jesus expects from his people?

3. Jesus condemns two things in Matthew 5:27-28: the lustful look and the adulterous act. For what reasons? Do you agree with Jesus? Explain your position.

4. Genesis 1:27 says that God created humans as male and female in his own image. What are the implications of this statement regarding male and female sexuality?

5. One way to interpret Jesus' ministry in general and the Sermon on the Mount specifically is that Jesus wanted to restore things to the Creator's original intention. In what way does Jesus' teaching about sexuality point to that?

6. The apostles followed up on Jesus' teaching in the New Testament congregations. A frequent motif in their teaching was that Christians belong to the Lord, they are united with him. To understand what that means for human sexuality, study 1 Corinthians 6:12-20; then answer these questions: (a) What is the body for? (b) What is it not for? (c) What is the result of sexual intercourse with a prostitute?

7. First Corinthians 6:18 includes this statement: "All other sins a man commits are outside his body, but he who sins sexually sins against his own body." Are sexual sins a unique category? In what way are they against the body?

8. Does the Bible view sexuality as a positive or as a negative part of personhood? Is it good or bad? Does the Bible's teaching agree with the way you were taught?

Sexuality and Wholeness

Sexuality is the second subject Jesus spoke about using this expression: "You have heard that it was said. . . . But I tell you." In Jesus' instructions about the relationship between men and women, he spoke of adultery, lustful desire, and adultery in the heart. Clearly, he was speaking to men—which brings up the question of whether sexuality is more of a problem for men than for women. Or was Jesus speaking directly to the men because that was the custom of his culture? Would he speak in the same way now?

In raising the issue of sexuality, Jesus touched a vital dynamic in human experience, although it may not have been as consuming an issue then as it is now. Today we certainly need help to cope with the issue. Changes related to sexuality are numerous, such as a preoccupation with sex, the so-called sexual revolution, women's liberation, with changing role expectations for men and women, marital disintegration, sexually transmitted diseases, the prevalence of abortion, and agitation for the acceptance of homosexuality.

We are confronted by a tidal wave of change that almost makes one despair as to whether traditional values will survive. It seems to me that the present situation makes Jesus' teaching about sexuality more, rather than less, important. If the way we handle our sexuality is to be conducive to wholeness, it will happen only by conforming to the principles that Jesus taught. To be salt and light to today's world will demand commitment to the Lord's will. It will require willingness to get into vigorous dialogue in the church about how to follow Jesus' teaching about sexuality.

Vladimir Lenin, a major force behind the Soviet Revolution of 1917, had a "glass of water" theory about sex. He believed that sex is as insignificant morally and emotionally as taking a drink when one is thirsty. It was a ghastly miscalculation, of course. He should have known that because of sex kings have abandoned their thrones, saints have abandoned their faith, and spouses their marriages. The communists also soon abandoned the glass-of-water notion about sex.

It has been noted many times that there is a revolution going on in sexual standards. In our country it is true that there are practically no restrictions as long as sexual activity is between consenting adults. However, some say that the revolution is either winding down or has already ended. The March 1983 issue of *Reader's Digest* carried an article by George Leonard, "The End of Sex," in which he claims that America's love affair with sex has run its course. He contrasts sex, a relatively worthless activity, with love, a rich and beautiful experience achievable in a lifelong relationship between husband and wife. Leonard thinks that using the term *sex* as a synonym for *love* is a distortion and should be discarded. *Time*

magazine (4 April 1984) carried a similar article entitled "The Revolution Is Over."

For people whose intention was to obey Jesus regarding
sexuality, there never was a revolution. For them it made little difference what changes the world was making. The call for obedience
to Jesus remained the same, and the standard for their lives
remained the same.

I am in solidarity with those Christians who wish to align their
position squarely with Jesus' teaching about sexuality. In one-night
stands a man and woman may have sex together, but it is a perversion of sexuality that is too close to the glass-of-water theory. Marriage provides a setting where husband and wife can mature in a
relationship that God blesses. It is an indictment of the entertain-
ment industry in our culture that it succeeds in making wholesome-
ness and purity appear quaint while the tawdry and cheap is portrayed as appealing. That kind of sex may look appealing, but in the
long run engaging in it is like being struck by a venomous snake.

Within reasonable limits a positive outcome of the sexual revolution is a greater freedom to be frank in discussing sexuality. In a
network television interview, Father Theodore Hesburgh, president
of the University of Notre Dame, spoke about his sexuality. He was
free to admit that he is attracted to women although he is celibate.
That appears to be a model of honesty worth following. The frank-
ness of some people, however, is tasteless and not within reasonable
boundaries.

Human sexuality is a gift of the Creator. But the gift so readily
lends itself to perversion and abuse that it would be easy to slip into
cynicism about sexuality. Sexual conduct that departs from biblical
standards is full of booby traps. A review of some of these traps un-
derlines the statement by Paul in 1 Corinthians 6:18: "He who sins
sexually sins against his own body." In light of all the ills following
in the wake of the sexual revolution, Paul's view sounds like rock-
ribbed truth. Here are some of the results of uncontrolled sexuality

Venereal disease (increasingly called sexually transmitted diseases). Until recently it was assumed that syphilis would be eradi-
cated. Now it is on the rise again. Herpes is another one of the
scourges of the sexual revolution that has injected a new soberness
into thinking about sexuality. AIDS (Acquired Immune Deficiency

Syndrome) appeared recently among practicing homosexuals. It is reaching epidemic levels and has spread to other people. Jesus' sexual standard would eradicate sexually transmitted diseases.

Female infertility has greatly increased since 1965. Analysis of causes is still under way, but the culprit appears to be sexually transmitted diseases.

Child pornography and child molestation. Twisted sexuality has a vicious side. The suffering of innocent children is an example. In January 1985, Cleveland authorities announced the cracking of a child pornography ring. In other places adults have been guilty of sexually molesting children in day-care centers.

Broken hearts, broken marriages, broken homes—and the emotional upheavals that follow for parents and children. Irresponsible sexuality carries an exorbitant price tag.

Reverence is offered to God because of who he is and for what he has created, especially human personality. Sexuality is an integral part of self-identity. Male and female are created in the image of God. Therefore, we are called to have reverence for every person— an attitude difficult to maintain but utterly essential for wholeness of life.

One Sabbath a crippled woman was in the synagogue where Jesus was teaching. She had been crippled for eighteen years and could not stand straight at all. When Jesus saw her, he touched her and she immediately straightened up. In contrast, modern attitudes about sexuality are so perverse that when they touch a woman she immediately becomes "crooked."

E. Stanley Jones uses the phrase "reverence for personality"— apropos in regard to sexuality. The biblical equivalent for "reverence for personality" is *love.* "You shall love your neighbor as yourself" is the earthly measure of whether we love God. Reverence for personality is the focus throughout Matthew 5:21-48. It undergirds the teaching about anger, murder, and feelings of contempt. The teaching about adultery and lust is rich in reverence for the personhood of each man and woman.

Jesus took the commandment "Do not commit adultery" and shifted it so that men have to face their inner attitudes about women. Is a woman's value in being a sex object? That is the "crookedness" imposed on women by pornography and lust. Is not a woman's value in having been created, equally with man, in God's image?

Distorted sexuality leads to the tearing down of men and women. A growing phenomenon in some places, such as Minneapolis and Indianapolis, is the view of pornography as a violation of women's civil rights. In both cities women have been working to obtain city statutes that would ban pornography on the grounds that it is a civil rights violation. Is such thinking parallel to reverence for personality?

Application to Life

It is easier to say what the rules for sexual conduct should be than it is to live by them, especially when Jesus includes our heart attitudes. In addition to the Word of God and the indwelling Holy Spirit, we have as a resource the body of Christ. Is there not strength in a common agreement to obey the Lord? Members must be ready to encourage each other to follow the Lord's will. The church must also be ready to offer those who fail a new beginning.

What other resources are available for people who wish to follow Jesus Christ and experience sexuality as a blessing?

Additional Study Resources

Driver, 84-86; Jones, 146-54; Miller, 50; *IDB,* 'Heart', 'Sex, Sexual Behavior' and 'Woman'; *ZPEB,* 'Sex' and 'Woman'.

Notes

_____

_____

_____

_____

_____

_____

_____

_____

_____

IT HAS BEEN SAID, "Anyone who divorces his wife must give her a certificate of divorce." But I tell you that anyone who divorces his wife, except for marital unfaithfulness, causes her to commit adultery, and anyone who marries a woman so divorced commits adultery.

Matthew 5:31-32

7

Marriage, Divorce, and Remarriage

JESUS' WORD about marital failure is the third of four teachings he introduced by contrasting them with what had been said before on these issues. Each of the four teachings concerns a vital discipleship issue. That means each of the four intersects with the way we live.

One way to interpret the lesson text is to view it as a continuation of the previous passage about sexuality. Both passages refer to adultery. It is as though Jesus said to the Jews, "You vigorously condemn adultery as a violation of God's law, but then you twist the law to allow divorce so that you can commit adultery anyway."

The focus for this session is divorce and remarriage—what Jesus and the apostles said about these issues, the position of the Mennonite Church, and the meaning of forgiveness when a marriage fails.

Exploring the Text

1. The issue of divorce is of great significance to the Christian community. Jesus' teaching about it makes that quite clear. His statement in Matthew 5:31 is based on Deuteronomy 24:1. Instead of a direct quote, Jesus gave a summary of 24:1. Why did he not quote?

Did he change the essence of the Old Testament passage?

2. Jesus began his restatement of Deuteronomy 24:1 with the word *anyone*. There is a special significance in his use of this term. Turn to Exodus 21:12-17, where the word *anyone* (NIV) appears four times to introduce four violations. Why do you suppose Jesus used the *anyone* formula?

Note that each violation has a penalty attached. However, Jesus did not attach a penalty to his statement. Why do you think he omitted it? What does the omission mean for us?

3. Deuteronomy 24:1 was the Old Testament text used by the Jews as their guide for divorce and remarriage questions. In Jesus' time, there were two well-known ways to interpret the text, and each interpretation had a strong following: (a) Rabbi Shamai said, "Divorce is allowed only in the case of adultery." (b) Rabbi Hillel said, "Divorce is allowed for any and every reason." Which interpretation corresponds more nearly to Deuteronomy 24:1? How could there be such divergent interpretations?

4. In light of the two schools of interpretation, what was the implication for Jesus of the Pharisees' test question in Matthew 19:3-9?

5. In his response to the Pharisees, what did Jesus point out as the basis for all divorce and remarriage questions?

6. The Pharisees asked Jesus why Moses commanded the giving of divorce certificates? Did Moses command it? What basis have you for your answer?

7. What is the significance of Matthew 19:3-9 for people in your congregation who may be considering divorce as an option?

8. What are the implications of 19:10-12 for people considering marriage as an option?

9. In Matthew 5:31-32 Jesus ties adultery and divorce together. Do you agree with his statement? What about it makes you uneasy?

10. The social, economic, and legal status of women was lower in those days. What effect would Jesus' teaching, if obeyed, have had on the status of women?

Marriage, Purity, and Forgiveness

Like other human relationships, marriage has a long history of failures mixed with successes. Forgiveness comes into the picture at the point of failure. That brings us to the realities that God's people face in regard to marriage: God's ideal is one man and one woman in lifelong union. There is also the sad fact of marital failure, requiring forgiveness. The marriage ideal may be pure and holy, but it does not exceed the high and pure ideal of forgiveness.

No less a man than Abraham and his family knew failure and needed forgiving grace. Abraham divorced Hagar and sent her away with their son Ishmael. The divorce happened because of Sarah's emphatic demand: "Get rid of that slave woman and her son" (Genesis 21:10). Sarah's anger was obvious, as was the anguish it precipitated. Deserted by family and excluded from the protection of home and clan, Hagar wandered in the desert with fourteen-year-old Ishmael. When their water supply was exhausted and Ishmael was near death, an angel intervened to save them. The harshness of failure was softened by an act of grace. Unfortunately, the narrative does not indicate whether Abraham and Sarah also received the grace of forgiveness.

Many divorced women today wander in a social desert that does not fully accept unmarried mothers. They wander in an economic desert, unable to furnish adequate support for their children because they do not have the necessary skills to find employment that pays above minimum wage. The social and economic pressure on them to remarry is enormous.

Marital problems and divorce also were common in Jesus' time. He spoke about divorce so pointedly that it jolted people. In light of the heavy demands in his teaching, the disciples wondered whether it might be better never to marry (Matthew 19:10).

Marriage and divorce is an important issue in the community of faith. That is as true today as it was in Jesus' day. The importance he attached to it is indicated by the way he spoke about divorce. Here are the five basic New Testament statements about divorce and remarriage:

Luke 16:18—Anyone who divorces his wife and marries another woman commits adultery, and the man who marries a divorced woman commits adultery.

Mark 10:11-12—Anyone who divorces his wife and marries another woman commits adultery against her. And if she divorces her husband and marries another man, she commits adultery.

Matthew 5:32—Anyone who divorces his wife, except for marital unfaithfulness, causes her to commit adultery, and anyone who marries a woman so divorced commits adultery.

Matthew 19:9—Anyone who divorces his wife, except for marital unfaithfulness, and marries another woman commits adultery.

First Corinthians 7:10-11—A wife must not separate from her husband. But if she does, she must remain unmarried or else be reconciled to her husband. And a husband must not divorce his wife.

Jesus' disciples were astonished at the implications of his teaching: "If this is the situation between a husband and wife, it is better not to marry" (Matthew 19:10). Their observation may have been correct, at least for some people. But more significantly, their surprise lets us know that Jesus' message about marriage sounded revolutionary.

Was his message revolutionary? One way to look at it is to think about our own situation. If Jesus' word were followed, what would change? It seems to me the change would be as dramatic as it was in the first century. When Jesus' disciples created new faith communities, a new way of living emerged. Here are some of the changes that resulted from Jesus' teaching: (a) Sexuality was elevated to a higher plane, reducing the occurrence of destructive practices; (b) in the churches women and men could freely associate without fear of losing their spouses; (c) the status of women rose from chattel and sex object to valued person sharing equally the grace of God; (d) the rate of divorce and remarriage decreased; (e) people experienced forgiveness.

"At one time Mennonites were known for their solid, stable marriages and families. Then they caught up with twentieth-century America, and it was no longer so," says Abraham Schmitt, a marriage counselor in eastern Pennsylvania ("Mennonite Marriages: Till Divorce Do Us Part?" *Christian Living,* February 1979). Schmitt characterizes Mennonite marriages this way: "When they are good, they are very, very good; when they are bad, they are horrid." Those that are horrid become that way because of suppressed emotions and unresolved conflict. Handling conflict and emotions is a basic task in building enduring relationships. Failing to deal with conflict and negative emotions ruins marriages.

It is helpful to know the history of the Mennonite Church regarding attempts to follow Jesus' teaching on marriage, divorce and remarriage. The following historical summary is the pilgrimage of our denomination. The value of this history lies not in whether it is better than that of any other denomination but in that it shows the struggle of one people trying to walk the path of discipleship in marriage.

1. The Mennonite Church had its beginnings in 1525 in Zurich, Switzerland. Already in 1527 the Swiss Brethren (Anabaptists) printed a tract in which they said that the "exception clause" in Matthew 5:32 and 19:9 confers on the innocent spouse the right to remarry. "Jesus permitted remarriage for only one reason, marital infidelity."

2. Menno Simons wrote in a similar vein.

3. From 1690 to 1867 the Mennonite Church generally did not allow remarriage.

4. From the Civil War to 1900 marriage was viewed as permanent, but divorced and remarried persons who asked for membership generally were received as members. For example, an 1867 Virginia Conference report says: "It was decided that for the same reason that a man is allowed to put away his wife, he is allowed to marry again."

In 1875 the Indiana Conference noted that since a brother who had married a divorced woman had known the requirements of the gospel, as well as the rules of the church, he had committed "a very serious transgression." However, they decided, "If he truly repents and brings forth fruits meet for repentance, he can be received again according to 1 Corinthians 6:9-11."

George Weaver, a bishop of Lancaster Conference from 1854 to 1883, tolerated a man in the church "who was living with another man's wife." She evidently was divorced.

In 1887, church leaders of Franconia Conference decided that a man who had married a divorced woman could be received into the Towamencin congregation if the members approved unanimously.

5. From 1900 to about 1950, under the influence of Daniel Kauffman, divorced and remarried people were not accepted into fellowship. Living with a divorced person was viewed as a sin.

6. Since 1950 the church has generally followed the model of the Swiss Brethren and that of 1865-1900.

A significant factor in the Mennonite response to Jesus' teaching is that we have been walking a tightrope. With mixed results we have tried to balance ourselves between two equally demanding, equally radical, requirements: one, make marriage measure up to the ideal of a lifelong monogamous union; two, make good the offer of unlimited forgiveness to those who fail. The aim was to avoid being both rigid and legalistic about lifelong unions and irresponsible about failure. Any group that attempts to avoid these extremes occasionally will lean too far in either direction—legalism or easy forgiveness. Clearly this has been the experience of the Mennonite Church, as the historical summary above shows.

Legalism or grace—which one governs what we think and say about marriage, marital problems, divorce and remarriage? Jesus' position on the issues seems strict and inflexible. There were reasons for that. One was that he was appealing for a return to the Creator's original intention (Matthew 19:4-6). Another was the inconsistency of the Jews who used the Law to teach that adultery was wrong (Exodus 20:14)—they prized their sexual purity—but then circumvented the Law by loosening the divorce rules so that, in effect, they could commit adultery anyway (Matthew 19:3, 7).

Christians who sincerely intend to live by the will of Jesus sometimes fail in marriage. When this happens, the spouses experience strong emotions: a sense of failure, frustration, rejection, anger, vindictiveness, loss of worth, and guilt. The emotions are overpowering and leave deep wounds. Those wounds are major contributors to the excessively high failure rate of second marriages—over 70 percent according to some observers. The situation is so serious that some secular marriage counselors now say a second marriage should not be entered into for at least five years after divorce. It may be that we need to be jolted so that we join the disciples in saying that if that is the situation, it is better not to marry (again). However, forgiveness means that if the old wounds are healed, if an individual has confessed his or her sin, if there is acceptance of personal responsibility for the sin of divorce, if the immaturities that caused the failure have been left behind, then forgiveness includes the offer of a new beginning.

Application to Life

1. The marriage scene is a mess in our culture. Does Jesus' teaching have relevance for us? Can congregations expect people to live by Jesus' high standard?

2. What is your congregation's position on marriage, divorce, and remarriage? Do you have a strong teaching program to help marriages mature? Is it safe to talk about the issues in your congregation?

3. Forgiveness may be even more difficult to practice than marital wholeness and permanence. How well do you do personally in offering unlimited forgiveness? Does your congregation practice it? What is irresponsible forgiveness?

Additional Study Resources

Driver, 86-90; Jones, 154-57; Miller, 50-57; Wenger, *Dealing Redemptively; Mennonite Confession of Faith*, Article 15; *IDB* and *ZPEB*, 'Divorce' and 'Marriage'.

Notes

_____

_____

_____

_____

_____

_____

_____

_____

_____

_____

_____

_____

_____

AGAIN, YOU HAVE heard that it was said to the people long ago, "Do not break your oath, but keep the oaths you have made to the Lord." But I tell you, Do not swear at all: either by heaven, for it is God's throne; or by the earth, for it is his footstool; or by Jerusalem, for it is the city of the Great King. And do not swear by your head, for you cannot make even one hair white or black. Simply let your "Yes" be "Yes," and your "No," "No"; anything beyond this comes from the evil one.

Matthew 5:33-37

8

The Oath
of Truthfulness

WHEN COMPARED to issues related to sexuality and marriage, the issue of truthfulness and swearing oaths may seem uninteresting and less important. However, it is a vital issue, on a par with the other lifestyle issues about which Jesus taught.

People who bring anger, sexuality, and marriage into the arena of discipleship bring their speech into the same arena. Once these are recognized as discipleship issues, it becomes clear that the issue is living by the Lord's word.

The life-related focus of our text is the question of what is the best way to promote truthfulness in human communication. All nations and all social groups face the issue, and all of them turn to the oath to promote truthfulness. Jesus recognized the need for truthfulness. He also acknowledged the universal use of the oath. Then he gave a joltingly different directive: "Do not swear at all."

Exploring the Text

1. It is not clear which Old Testament passage Jesus was referring to when he said, "Again, you have heard that it was said to the people long ago." Perhaps it was Ecclesiastes 5:4: "When you make a vow to God, do not delay in fulfilling it." Do you think Jesus was setting

aside or negating the Old Testament? What was the relationship of Jesus' teaching to the Old Testament?

2. Jesus' statement "Do not swear at all" raises a problem of biblical interpretation. In the Scriptures, God, as well as the saints, sometimes uses an oath. Why, for example, does God swear by himself in Genesis 22:15-18? Does Hebrews 6:16-18 give a different viewpoint than Jesus' command not to swear at all? If, as Hebrews 6:16 says, "the oath . . . puts an end to all argument," how is that accomplished?

3. How do you understand Exodus 20:7? Does it refer to profanity, swearing oaths in God's name, or what?

4. What is the issue or conflict in Exodus 22:10-13? How was it to be resolved?

5. In Psalm 110:4a, how does God follow through when he swears?

6. According to Ecclesiastes 5:4-7, what may be the outcome of a human oath? In light of this passage, does Hebrews 6:16 need to be modified?

7. In Matthew 5:33-37 Jesus mentioned four things that people commonly swore by. What were they?

8. The Jews were tempted to, and frequently did, swear frivolously and evasively. Any oath using God's name was considered binding, because it made God a partner in the transaction. Any oath not using God's name was not considered binding, because God was not part of the transaction. What point was Jesus making by listing the four things that people commonly swore by? Can God be left out of any transaction?

9. Read Matthew 26:69-75. Here is the well-known story of Peter's denial of his Lord. Less well-known is the fact that the denial moved through three traditionally used levels of authentication of a statement: (a) denial (v. 70), (b) denial with an oath (v. 72), (c) denial with a curse (v. 74). Which level gave the most authenticity to Peter's denial?

Ways to Uphold Truth and Stop Lies

"Do you swear to tell the truth, the whole truth, and nothing but the truth, so help you God?" Legal hearings and court proceedings normally ask witnesses to take an oath of truthfulness. Then testimony is entered into the official record. If the witness gives deliberately false testimony, then she or he is guilty of perjury.

Public officials customarily take an oath of office with one hand on a Bible and the other raised. They solemnly swear to faithfully carry out the duties of office according to prescribed procedures.

Mennonites, Quakers, and some others customarily refuse to swear an oath because Jesus said, "Do not swear at all. . . . Simply let your 'Yes' be 'Yes,' and your 'No,' 'No'; anything beyond this comes from the evil one."

George Fox, a Quaker leader, was as widely known for his truthfulness as some are for their lack of it. People said of him, "If George Fox says 'Verily,' there is no altering him." The goal of requiring oaths is to help people do as Fox did.

Apparently all nations view swearing as necessary to control falsehood. The United States takes a flexible position. Although the oath is used, the U.S. Constitution recognizes the conscience of people against swearing and guarantees them freedom from having to take an oath. In hearings or in legal documents, citizens may opt to affirm rather than swear.

People use various expressions to emphasize what they say. Fox did it with his "Verily"—a practice he copied from Jesus. The expressions people use today to underscore a point are frivolous swearing. Here are some examples: "I swear to God"; "I did not do it—honest to God"; "God is my witness"; "No lie"; "So help me, God"; "I swear I'll do it"; "Trust me." Frivolous oaths carry no legal weight. That may be why legal oaths are called for with a question using the word *solemnly*.

There was frivolous and evasive swearing in Jesus' time too. The practice is evident in his reference to the four things people commonly swore by (Matthew 5:34-36). The Jews frivolous swearing had two underlying assumptions: (1) Any oath using God's name was considered binding, because it made God a partner in the transaction. (2) Any oath not using God's name was not considered binding—not even if it was by heaven, earth, Jerusalem, or one's own head. The Jews said that God was not part of such a transaction.

Jesus' response to their swearing was to point out that God is involved in all human transactions, regardless of whether or not God's name is used. Ploys to include or exclude God are fantasies that undermine spiritual wholeness. People are immature when they say God is present in one part of life and absent in another.

We should be clear about Jesus' purpose in saying, "Do not swear at all." We should also understand why governments employ the oath. Both seek to promote truthfulness, but the means to the end are diametrically opposed because the underlying assumptions are radically different. The assumption in using the oath is that life can be compartmentalized. When under oath, a person likely will tell the truth rather than face the penalties of perjury. When not under oath, the person cannot be depended on to tell the truth unless it is convenient.

The assumption behind Jesus' position is that life cannot be compartmentalized and to attempt to do so is destructive. God is present in all human transactions. Therefore, believers should always speak the truth. Use of the oath suggests this attitude: "Now that I am forced to it, I will tell the truth; otherwise I might not." Jesus' followers who reject the use of oaths are making several positive affirmations:

(1) God is present to all human transactions.

(2) It is possible to establish a community of faith where telling the truth is a firm and assumed practice.

(3) In the church, truth is not imposed on liars by use of oaths. The church is more like ex-liars whose minds have been transformed. For Christians truth flows from inner integrity, from inner consistency.

Above all . . . do not swear"—so wrote James in 5:12. "The oath is a right good work, by which God is praised; the truth and right are confirmed and lies are stopped"—so wrote Martin Luther, who made no secret about his dislike for James' epistle. Luther's position regarding the Sermon on the Mount was that it was not for public life; and that took care of the oath, which is used precisely in public life.

It is essential to keep three facts straight: One, all governments use the oath to uphold the truth and stop lies. Two, Jesus had the same goal but without the oath. Three, the assumptions of Jesus and the state are at variance. The state assumes that the penalties of perjury will make people tell the truth. Jesus assumed that his people, having tasted new life in the kingdom, will freely tell the truth.

The Quakers were one group who set out to uphold the truth and stop lies without the oath. We owe them a debt of appreciation. Quaker merchants, because of their insistence on truthfulness, originated uniform pricing of merchandise. The price was always the same regardless of who the customer was.

In a rare display of unity, Mennonites all over the world have refused to take the oath. They sometimes paid dearly for that refusal. In 1769 Jacob Frey, a French Mennonite, refused to take the oath. He was fined ten pounds plus court costs and banished from France for life.

Application to Life

1. Do you understand Jesus' teaching about swearing oaths? What is your response to it? Which is the way to uphold truth and stop lying—the way of governments or the way of Jesus?

2. What person have you known who stands out as a model of simply telling the truth? For me it was my father. Once he gave his word—always simply "yes" or "no"—he was bound by it. An oath would have been superfluous. What would change in your community if Jesus' teaching were followed?

Additional Study Resources

Barclay, 90-91; Jones, 158-68; Miller, 57-59; *IDB* and *ZPEB*, 'Oath' and 'Truth'; *Mennonite Encyclopedia,* 'Oath'.

Notes

_____

_____

_____

_____

_____

_____

YOU HAVE HEARD that it was said, "Eye for eye, and tooth for tooth." But I tell you, Do not resist an evil person. If someone strikes you on the right cheek, turn to him the other also. And if someone wants to sue you and take your tunic, let him have your cloak as well. If someone forces you to go one mile, go with him two miles. Give to the one who asks you, and do not turn away from the one who wants to borrow from you.

Matthew 5:38-42

9

Retaliation

DOES IT WORK to turn the other cheek if someone slaps you? In what way, if any, is a community or the world improved when someone refuses to retaliate? Most people seem to doubt that Jesus' teaching about revenge is going to work as a rule for life. The question arises: What will happen to a person or a group of people who decide to take Jesus' teaching seriously and avoid revenge? More than most of us are willing to believe, the world tries to make a go of it by using retaliation and punishment. The focus of this lesson is the following question: Which way will we achieve the best results in life—by following "an eye for an eye" or "Do not resist an evil person"?

Exploring the Text

There are three options for responding to a person who has insulted, injured, or otherwise wronged you. All three appear in the Bible.

1. The first response is unlimited retaliation. Read Genesis 4:19-24. What wrong had Lamech experienced? What did he do about it? What was his position regarding retaliation? How do Peter's and Jesus' positions in Matthew 18:21-22 differ from

Lamech's? Do you know anyone who believes in unlimited retaliation?

2. The second option is limited retaliation. Read Exodus 21:22-25. What injury is spoken of? How was such a case to be resolved? Who had the final word in determining the penalty?

3. Read Deuteronomy 25:17-19. What wrong was done? Was the response to be unlimited or limited retaliation?

4. The limited retaliation option is often called the *law of the talion* (from Latin, *lex talionis*). The Jewish rabbis promoted it. What safeguards in Deuteronomy prevented personal and excessive use of it? Where have you seen it used?

5. Jesus presented a third option—no retaliation (Matthew 5:38-42). What is to be the response (a) if someone strikes you on the right cheek, (b) if someone wants to sue you, (c) if you are forced to go a mile with someone, (d) if someone asks something of you, (e) if someone asks for a loan?

6. E. Stanley Jones and others have pointed out that Jesus was not recommending passive resistance but active resistance. Which do you think better describes Jesus' position? In what ways are the five examples active resistance?

7. Is "no retaliation" an appropriate description of Jesus' position? What would be a better description? Read Romans 12:17-21. What additional help does Paul give for understanding the no-retaliation option?

A Redemptive Response to Evil

There is a deeply rooted punishment mentality in people. Some recent, unsettling data about how parents relate to their children said that the average parents spend fourteen minutes daily in dialogue with their children. Two minutes on neutral topics, and twelve haranguing them: "Don't do that." "You shouldn't have done that." "Clean up your room." "Why don't you get better grades?"

That kind of parenting comes from the notion that punishment is the bottom line of life. This notion assumes that sooner or later retribution will come to the evil person; and if it does not, then life is unfair. It assumes that fear of punishment is what makes an orderly community possible, that without it anarchy results. It assumes that the world turns on the principle of an eye for an eye and a tooth for a tooth. It assumes that when punishment is equivalent to the wrong done, then things have been made right.

The punishment mentality is seen in people's response to herpes, an incurable disease transmitted through sexual contact. Brent Deck, a 32-year-old engineer in Massachusetts, has the disease. He thought it was time to get herpes victims together, so he started New Day, a herpes dating service. One New Day member said, "I've been celibate for the last three years. It's like a deep, dark secret. There's isolation and withdrawal. Is this my time of hell on earth?"

In an article "Is Sex Dead?" (*New York,* 6 December 1982), Fran R. Schumer wrote, "Overnight, herpes has sobered a generation that oral contraceptives freed from second thoughts. Among . . . its effects herpes has returned sex to its former shading of corruption and guilt; it's viewed as the mark of an angry God punishing people for the sins of the sexual revolution."

There again is the assumption that the world is based on legal justice, every wrong requiring an equal punishment. Inevitably God is brought into the picture as the originator of the supposedly universal principle. Schumer's statement demonstrates that too.

Is that the way the universe is constituted? Does God respond to evil people on the basis of legal justice—the only difference between God's legal justice and ours being that God's is more just? After all, when Paul preached to the philosophers in the Areopagus, he said, "For he has set a day when he will judge the world with justice by the man he has appointed" (Acts 17:31). If Paul was speaking of legal justice, then we are faced with the question of which kind. Will it be what Lamech asserted for himself—unlimited retaliation? Most people would balk at that.

Another and far more common view of how God has constituted the universe is that it is grounded in *lex talionis*, the principle that when there is an exact meting of punishment for the evil done, then justice prevails—an eye for an eye and a tooth for a tooth. Undoubtedly, *lex talionis* was a great improvement over Lamech's position. Jewish justice was based on *lex talionis*, a system of limited retribution in case of injury or loss. Canadian and U.S. legal structures are based on the same idea. Most individuals support that principle and want it used to right the wrongs against them.

"Do not resist an evil person." Do we dare to assume that this is the way God responds to evil people? If so, is the universe grounded in something other than legal justice? Some people say that certainly God relates to evil people on the basis of grace, but human society cannot operate that way. God has his way; we have to have ours, they reason. But I like to think that Jesus' statement "Do not resist an evil person" was really an invitation for us to align our practice with the basic principle of our universe—love, not legal justice. Our practice is to be consistent with how God relates to us and not argue that it does not work. It will not work if no one tries it.

Paul's statement to the philosophers that God "will judge the world with justice" would surely seem to promote legal justice if Paul had not added more: "By the man he has appointed. He has given proof of this to all men by raising him from the dead." To interpret Paul's statement, two things need to be remembered: One, God did not respond to the evil of the Messiah's death by punishing the perpetrators. He redeemed the situation by raising Jesus from the dead. Two, the world is to be judged by Jesus—which means on the basis of forgiveness. All the requirements of justice are met in forgiveness. The way to redeem evil people is not by punishing but by forgiving them. When a murderer is executed, he or she is not redeemed nor is the victim brought back. But if the murderer is rehabilitated and can take a useful place in life, justice has been done.

In her book *Peace Be with You*, Cornelia Lehn tells the story of Que Huong and her husband, Ngoc Phuong. The couple lived in Saigon during the terrible civil war when the Thieu government and the revolutionary forces allowed no middle ground. Since Que and Ngoc could not join the violence of either side, both sides viewed them as enemies. Thieu's police arrested the couple, and in the torture that followed, Ngoc died.

After the war ended, someone asked Que what she would do if she met their torturer. She answered, "To be honest with you, there will be a little flame of anger inside of me which will want to flare up. But I've got to control it, because if I would kill him, his family would take revenge on me, and then my family would take revenge on them, and it would never end. But the cycle of hatred must stop."

Application to Life

1. Was Que Huong justified in her willingness to absorb the injustice and hostility? Were she and Ngoc Phuong justified in refusing to join either side?

2. What experiences have you had in which you struggled with whether to resist or not? Which of the five examples Jesus gives in Matthew 5:38-42 poses the most difficulty for you?

3. What is the bottom line in God's universe—legal justice or grace? Is the world or your neighborhood improved when someone does not retaliate? What should be the principle in families—punishment or forgiveness?

Additional Study Resources

Barclay, 160-67; Driver, 91-96; Jones, 169-96; Lehn, 106, 118; Miller, 59-61; Wenger, *Way of Peace,* 26-33; *ZPEB,* 'Retribution'.

Notes

_____

_____

_____

_____

_____

_____

_____

_____

_____

_____

_____

_____

_____

YOU HAVE HEARD that it was said, "Love your neighbor and hate your enemy." But I tell you: Love your enemies and pray for those who persecute you, that you may be sons of your Father in heaven. He causes his sun to rise on the evil and the good, and sends rain on the righteous and the unrighteous. If you love those who love you, what reward will you get? Are not even the tax collectors doing that? And if you greet only your brothers, what are you doing more than others? Do not even pagans do that? Be perfect, therefore, as your heavenly Father is perfect.

Matthew 5:43-48

10

Love Your Enemies

SIX TIMES Jesus contrasted his message with what had been taught in the past. In his teaching about loving the enemy is the sixth and last use of "You have heard . . . but I tell you." "Love your enemies" may well be the best known of all Jesus' teachings. Everyone knows about it, but few seem ready to practice it. That may mean that few understand its implications. At any rate, like Jesus' other hard sayings, this one deters many. The goal of this lesson is to come to terms with a hard saying.

Exploring the Text

1. Jesus' statement "Love your neighbor" was quoted from Leviticus 19:18. What other instructions are found in this verse?

2. Love for one's neighbor is important in the gospel. In our lesson text Jesus compares it with love for enemies. The parable of the good Samaritan (Luke 10:25-37) gives valuable clues for understanding Jesus' thinking about the neighbor issue. What must one do to inherit eternal life? What is the essential meaning of *neighbor*?

3. According to Matthew 5:43-48, did Jesus suggest that loving one's neighbor is in some sense deficient (vv. 46-47)? If it is deficient, what is the deficiency?

4. What point was Jesus making in the reference to the sun and rain? How does that statement support the command "Love your enemies"?

5. How does God relate to people? How do you want God to relate to you? Think of the person toward whom you feel most hostile. How do you want God to relate to that individual?

6. What is wrong with greeting only one's brother or sister?

7. The second part of the command says, "Pray for those who persecute you." How did Jesus do that? (See Luke 23:34.) How did Stephen do it? (See Acts 7:59-60.)

8. Is "Hate your enemies" a biblical statement? Where is it found? What are we to hate according to Psalm 97:10? According to Amos 5:15?

9. By implication, Matthew 5:43-48 makes humans God's enemies. Do you think that is true? According to Romans 5:6-8, how does God relate to us? How does God change enemies into friends?

The Lord's Command and Just War

The basic ethic for all human relationships is "Love your neighbor as yourself." Jesus' command "Love your enemies" builds on the basic ethic but broadens it to include the issue of using violence to settle disputes. The basic ethic is a sweeping statement. "Love your enemy" is more pointed, disallowing all recourse to war. However, the command is not simply a no to war and other violence. It is not merely an invitation to passivity. Rather, just as God provides sunshine and rain for the evil and good, so we are to bring blessings upon our enemies.

People often marvel at the open border between Canada and the United States. It could be very different except for the vision of two men. In *Peace Be with You*, Cornelia Lehn relates an international development in which fear and suspicion were set aside in favor of trust.

The War of 1812 was fought between the United States and Britain, and Canada was a British ally. After a peace treaty was signed, there was strong sentiment on both sides for arming the U.S.-Canadian border. Then Richard Rush, of the U.S. State Department, went to Sir Charles Bagot, who was in charge of Canadian affairs. Together they worked out a bold plan: (1) Each country would lets its soldiers go home. (2) All the battleships would withdraw from the Great Lakes. (3) All the forts along the U.S.-Canadian border would be destroyed.

While hostility between the two nations was high, many people supported the plan; and in 1817 the Rush-Bagot Agreement was signed. Ever since then, the 3,000-mile border has been unarmed; and differences have been resolved at the conference table, not on battlefields.

The method of biblical interpretation is inevitably part of the picture in serious discussion about war and peace. A particularly nettlesome and divisive issue in biblical interpretation is the relationship between the Old and New Testaments. "Flat book" advocates say that the two Testaments are equal in authority and that since God commanded Israel to fight in some instances Jesus clearly would not have decreed an end to all war-making.

Promise and fulfillment, an approach to biblical interpretation that appeals to Mennonites, views the Old Testament as setting the stage for the gospel of Christ. The Old Testament promises; the New fulfills. In this approach, the New Testament is the Christian's final authority. Therefore, Jesus' command "Love your enemies" supersedes any previous word.

Superficially, at least, to say that Jesus' teaching supersedes the Old Testament assumes a contrast between the two parts of the Bible. It is uncomfortable to be tagged with holding that position. Is there a framework within which to handle war-and-peace issues that lessens the distress of seemingly irreconcilable positions between the Testaments?

The concept of *holy war* may offer such a framework. The term is not used in the Bible, but the concept is. When God commanded Israel to destroy an evil enemy, it was God, not Israel, who declared war; and the power to win was God's, not Israel's. "The Lord is a warrior" (Exodus 15:5), sang Israel after crossing the Red Sea. When David faced Goliath, he said, "The battle is the Lord's" (1 Samuel 17:47). Similar statements appear repeatedly in the Old Testament.

While holy war ideas continued in the New Testament, they were reformulated and the battle was no longer against national enemies. It has become a spiritual struggle. "For though we live in the world, we do not wage war as the world does. The weapons we fight with are not the weapons of the world. On the contrary, they have divine power to demolish strongholds" (2 Corinthians 10:3-4). In his "armor of God" writing (Ephesians 6:10-18) Paul says, "For our struggle is not against flesh and blood, but against the rulers, against the authorities, against the powers of this dark world and against the spiritual forces of evil in the heavenly realms."

The warfare of the New Testament is against sin, and its outcome is dependent on the power of God; it still is holy war but of a very different sort from the days of Israel. The Christian's struggle is directed against the very source of humankind's warring. "The war to end wars" was the cry when the United States entered World War I in 1917. There is, in fact, a war to end wars, and it is waged by warriors who have laid aside bombs, bullets, bazookas, and bayonets. Their weapons are spiritual, and they call people to be reconciled to God and to each other. World War I spawned wars. Jesus and the apostles called people to spurn them.

There have been two traditions in church history regarding the Christian's response to war. One says that all war is evil, that we are to love our enemies, and that killing is certainly not the same as loving. An example of this position is this statement by Conrad Grebel: "Christians employ neither worldly sword nor war, since with them killing is absolutely renounced" (5 September 1524).

The other tradition says that Christians must fight for justice and against oppression. This is known as just-war theory. Here is a summary of the tradition: (1) A just war must have high motives. The reason for going to war is the restoration of peace, not anger or retaliation. (2) It is immoral to go to war unless success is reasonably certain. (3) Good effects must outweigh bad effects. (4) Immunity for noncombatants must be guaranteed.

A number of questions need to be raised here. Can any war be justified by just-war criteria? Can the factors in war be controlled so that the four points can be followed? Could a war using nuclear weapons be just? The just-war theory is more a justification by a church in Babylonian (or pagan) captivity for its militarism than a valid argument for the justness of some wars. Rationalization of self-contradictory conduct is an old trick. The church has done more than its fair share of this, trying simultaneously to exalt Jesus as Lord and to pay homage to Mars, the god of war.

For close to three centuries, from Christ to about A.D. 300, the church did not participate in wars—which, in itself, is an indication of the course set by Jesus and the apostles. The shift to participation in war in the fourth century resulted from two factors: (1) the success of the church in evangelizing the world and the church's accommodating to the world; (2) the influence and policies of Constantine as emperor of Rome from A.D. 312 and of the entire Roman Empire from 324 to 337.

Constantine issued an edict of toleration, making Christian worship lawful. His motivation was more shrewd politics than personal understanding of or agreement with the New Testament. Nevertheless, the church rushed to embrace Constantine. His policies became the policies of the church. A pagan warrior had conquered the church rather than being won by the gospel. It was a case of the church being shaped into the image of Constantine.

Constantine's reformulation of the gospel was evidenced in 312 at the battle of Milvian Bridge, where he defeated Maxentius, his rival. He reportedly saw a cross before the battle. Written on it were the words "By this sign you shall conquer." The cross became Constantine's battle symbol. From it no longer issued the words "Father, forgive them." The message now was that unless you submit to the cross, we will make our swords red with your blood. The blood of Christ was made to baptize the bloodletting drive for world domination. The cross of the Suffering Servant was hoisted over the structures of oppression to bless them.

When the church, in its sanctification of Constantinianism, began to justify war, it had turned from the power of the Holy Spirit to the power of the sword. Constantinianism was the Babylonian captivity of the church. From Constantine to 1985 most Christians have supported war, often in opposing armies, Christian slaughtering Christian.

In conclusion, it should be pointed out that avoidance of war is, by itself, too narrow. Avoidance of war is only one aspect of peacemaking. What is the scope of a peacemaker's activity? Here is a lovely answer to that question:

True evangelical faith cannot lie dormant;
it clothes the naked
it feeds the hungry
it comforts the sorrowful
it shelters the destitute
it serves those that harm it
it binds up that which is wounded
it has become all things to all men.
          —*Menno Simons, 1539*

Application to Life

1. Do you think "Love your enemies" means that Christians should refuse to join the military? Can any war be just?

2. How do you respond to Menno Simons' statement about true evangelical faith? In what ways can you put that into practice?

Additional Study Resources

Barclay, 170-77; Driver, 96-99; Gallardo, *Way of Biblical Justice;* Jones, 169-96: Jordan, 63-71; Lehn, 58; Miller, 61-64; Wenger, *Way of Peace; Mennonite Encyclopedia,* 'Nonresistance'.

Notes

_____
_____
_____
_____
_____
_____
_____
_____
_____
_____

BE CAREFUL not to do your "acts of righteousness" before men, to be seen by them. If you do, you will have no reward from your Father in heaven.

So when you give to the needy, do not announce it with trumpets, as the hypocrites do in the synagogues and on the streets, to be honored by men. I tell you the truth, they have received their reward in full. But when you give to the needy, do not let your left hand know what your right hand is doing, so that your giving may be in secret. Then your Father, who sees what is done in secret, will reward you.

Matthew 6:1-4

11

Giving to the Needy

SIX ISSUES have confronted us in the last six lessons of our study: anger, sexuality, divorce, oaths, retaliation, and love for enemies. These six issues are enmeshed in our living. They are always with us. The way Jesus taught about them compels us to listen. Anyone deciding to live by Jesus' teachings is confronted with a new way of relating to other people. The overarching question has been, "How do we abide by God's will in human relationships?"

In this lesson there is a shift of focus from direct consideration of human relationships to our relationship to God. Jesus explored the new focus in three ways that we express our piety: giving to the needy, prayer, and fasting. In this lesson we take up the first of these.

Exploring the Text

1. Jesus uses the phrase "acts of righteousness" in Matthew 6:1. What does the phrase mean? Is the definition given in verses 1-4?

2. Motives are the problem in this passage. How is the motive question raised in verse 1? How are motives viewed in verse 2? How is the motive issue addressed in verses 3-4?

3. There is no evidence that people in Jesus' time actually blew trumpets to announce their giving. It sounds like hyperbole and it sounds funny. Do you ever "have the trumpet blown"? Have you seen others do it? What part of human nature was Jesus speaking of?

4. How does the statement in verse 3—"Do not let your left hand know what your right hand is doing"—help us in assessing our motives?

5. Read Deuteronomy 15:7-11. Jesus' words in Matthew 6:1-4 are about motives, but the context is when we give to help the poor. The Old Testament provides rich background regarding almsgiving. According to Deuteronomy 15:7, how were people with means to relate to the poor? How would you describe the attitude toward the poor called for in 15:8?

6. What evil motivation is pointed to in Deuteronomy 15:9 (see vv. 1-2)?

7. What is to be the heart's intention according to Deuteronomy 15:10?

8. Read Deuteronomy 24:10-22. There were three different harvests each year in which provision was to be made for the poor. Name each harvest, and explain how the poor were cared for in each one.

9. What was to be Israel's motive for treating the poor with justice (see Deuteronomy 24:18)?

10. Do you affirm the cause of justice for the poor as outlined in the Bible? What about the reason given in Deuteronomy 24:19? Is that your motive in wanting to help the poor? Is it still a good motive?

11. Is there anything particularly evil about giving to the poor with impure motives?

Justice and Our Motivation

Justice for the poor, the motivation behind providing it, and the rewards for doing it—these are the three prongs of Matthew 6:1- 4. If a person gives alms to be seen doing it, according to Jesus, then the sought-after reward has been gained and the account is closed. That is a startling perception. The logic in it is hard to refute. If the motive is to have people see our piety, that can be achieved; but it is less certain that it will be appreciated by the onlookers. It is of course possible to hoodwink people, but God doesn't wink at such aims. God cannot be conned. Although it is possible to con others and even deceive oneself, eventually the reward matches the motivation.

Understanding Jesus' teaching is made easier if we realize how almsgiving developed during the intertestamental period—during the last several hundred years prior to Jesus' birth. Poverty was widespread, resulting in greater emphasis on almsgiving. Begging became an accepted profession, and giving to the poor was increasingly regarded as a pious act. Evidently, Israel's justice-for-the-poor heartbeat was skipping badly. The people no longer responded to the pure word, "There should be no poor among you. . . . Give to [the poor] as the Lord your God has blessed you. Remember that you were slaves in Egypt and the Lord your God redeemed you. That is why I give you this command today" (Deuteronomy 15:4, 14-15).

It was as though Israel's heart had been replaced with a mechanical one. The goal was no longer elimination but acceptance of poverty. The goal was not giving to rescue the poor from their condition but giving to redeem the giver. Almsgiving was assigned meritorious value, even able to atone for sin. Apocryphal literature, such as Tobit and Ecclesiasticus, includes clear statements presenting the new thinking: "Almsgiving delivers from death, and it will purge away every sin" (Tobit 12:9). That is not at all like the Lord's word in Deuteronomy 15:15 and 24:22.

These two texts from Deuteronomy actually point to three motives for helping the poor: (1) God commanded it, (2) because of God's saving mercy, (3) hope for reward. The God-model for helping the poor was the rescue of Israel from slavery in Egypt; so Israel was not to leave the poor trapped in poverty, doomed to beg. The God-model meant a new start for the poor. That motif is continued in the New Testament: People were enslaved by sin, poor and helpless; so God in Christ lifted their burden. There are the poor and helpless today; so we are to lift their burden.

During the intertestamental period, righteousness gradually came to be defined as almsgiving, prayer, and fasting. Almsgiving was regarded as the highest righteousness. That is why Jesus in-

troduced his teaching on those three practices by calling them "acts
of righteousness" (Matthew 6:1). Equating almsgiving with righteousness was common in Jesus' day, but it was out of joint with the
Law and cannot be squared with the gospel of Christ. In 2 Corinthians 9:9, Paul quotes Psalm 112:9: "He has scattered abroad his
gifts to the poor; his righteousness endures forever." Paul's point is
that giving is a grateful response to God by one already redeemed.
It does not justify anyone.

Jesus' teaching must be seen as a corrective to an evil twist—
the practice of giving to the needy for the reward of recognition and
as an effort to win atonement. The evil was in distorting the meaning of helping the poor as well as ruining one's relationship with
God.

Careful study of the Bible leads to the conclusion that, as already stated, almsgiving does not atone for sin—it is not righteousness in that sense. However, in Jesus' parable about the sheep and
the goats at the last judgment, the separation between the saved and
the damned hinges on whether one has performed acts of com-
passion for the needy: feeding the hungry, showing hospitality to
the stranger, giving clothes to the poor, caring for the ill, and visit-
ing prisoners (Matthew 25:31-46).

According to this parable, our eternal destiny depends not on
fame gained but on help given. If Jesus did not mean that care for
the poor is the means to salvation, then what did he mean? Here are
some conclusions that follow from the biblical teaching about com-
passion for the poor:

(1) Almsgiving does not justify sinners.

(2) It is righteousness in the sense that the redeemed help the
poor out of gratitude to God.

(3) Helping the poor is right conduct with enduring spiritual
value.

(4) One of the values of almsgiving is that is breaks the stran-
glehold of materialism.

(5) In the sheep and goats parable Jesus identified himself with
the world's poor. Doing good to the poor is the same as doing good
to him.

It is surprising how often rewards are mentioned in Jesus'
teachings about almsgiving. One such statement, which also relates

to the second conclusion above, is found in Mark 9:41: "I tell you the truth, anyone who gives you a cup of water in my name because you belong to Christ will certainly not lose his reward." The reward in question must be the same as in Matthew 25:34: "Come, you who are blessed by my Father; take your inheritance, the kingdom prepared for you."

Application to Life

Motives are tricky business, and a lifetime is too short to get them all sorted out so that you can be free from ego-centered drives. Therefore, the question is not whether you have arrived but whether you are on the way. At best, human existence is a matter of being in process. In Christ we are maturing, we are being redeemed, being liberated, being sanctified.

After having led a women's Bible study using these materials, Norma Godshall wrote: "After reading about the moral conduct expected in the kingdom, I know how impossible it is for me to be good. Jesus asks, 'Knowing this, why do you call yourself righteous?'

"Well, Lord, if I can't be good by your rules, could I at least be good in the eyes of others? At least I will receive their recognition. After all, Lord, there are a lot of people who do worse than I do. Look at Marlene. And then there is Joe. And what about Darlene?

"You may be right, my child, but I asked *you* the question. Are you doing good deeds so others will see and praise you? Get in the habit of giving because there is need, not because you want honor from others."

How can we work at distilling our motives?

Additional Study Resources

Barclay, 177-90; Driver, 100-105; Jones, 199-210; Jordan, 72-76; Miller, 66-71; Richardson, 'Poor'; *ZPEB,* 'Alms'.

Notes

BUT WHEN YOU pray, do not be like the hypocrites, for they love to pray standing in the synagogues and on the street corners to be seen by men. I tell you the truth, they have received their reward in full. When you pray, go into your room, close the door and pray to your Father, who is unseen. Then your Father, who sees what is done in secret, will reward you. And when you pray, do not keep on babbling like pagans, for they think they will be heard because of their many words. Do not be like them, for your Father knows what you need before you ask him.

This is how you should pray:
"Our Father in heaven,
hallowed be your name,
your kingdom come,
your will be done
on earth as it is in heaven.
Give us today our daily bread.
Forgive us our debts,
as we also have forgiven our debtors.
And lead us not into temptation,
but deliver us from the evil one.
For if you forgive men when they sin against you, your heavenly Father will also forgive you. But if you do not forgive men their sins, your Father will not forgive your sins.

Matthew 6:5-15

12

Prayer

PRAYER IS a basic element in worship whether it is private or public. Prayer is also a crucial factor in spiritual development. It is therefore not at all surprising that the Sermon on the Mount includes teaching about prayer. There are in fact two passages on prayer: the one covered in this lesson and the ask-seek-knock passage.

Jesus focused on three things in our lesson text: (1) people's motives when they pray, (2) a model prayer, (3) forgiveness.

Exploring the Text

1. In the matter of almsgiving the question was why give to the poor. Similarly, in the matter of prayer the question is why pray. Is it so that others hear and notice our piety? If not, then why?

2. Jesus assumed we achieve what we really want. What reward goes to those who want others to hear their prayers? What reward goes to those who really want God to hear them?

3. There are two negative prayer models in Matthew 6:5-8. What is the first, and what is wrong with it? What is the second model, and what is wrong with it?

4. There is a right place for prayer. Where is it, and what makes it the right place?

5. A number of questions arise out of verses 5-6 that need discussion: (a) What is the primary reward we should seek in prayer? (b) Why is private prayer a good practice? (c) How does the fact that God knows what we need before we ask affect your understanding of prayer?

6. The Lord's Prayer begins with the word *our,* a first-person plural pronoun. How many first-person plural pronouns are used in the prayer? What are the implications of praying that way?

7. What are the implications for human relationships of calling God "our Father"?

8. The Lord's Prayer focuses on two things. What is the focus in verses 9-10? in verses 11-13?

9. Jesus picked one theme out of the prayer for special emphasis. What was the theme? Why do you think he chose that one rather than another?

Unified Loyalty

James warned double-minded people to purify their hearts (James 4:8). Failure to find the wholeness to which Jesus invited people results from trying to face in two directions at once, from trying to gain the benefits of conflicting loyalties. That is double-mindedness. It conjures up a picture of straddling the fence.

E. Stanley Jones says that people's spiritual failures result from being inwardly divided. In *The Christ of the Mount* (p. 200), he lists nine expressions of human dividedness that Jesus pointed out:

(1) You do your beautiful religious acts with divided motives—you give to God, but also "to be seen of men" (6:1-4).

(2) You pray in two directions—to be heard of God and to be overheard of people (6:5-15).

(3) You fast with divided purpose—you do it before God and yet you hope that people will give you credit for being abstemious (6:16-18).

(4) You try to lay up treasure in two directions—upon earth and in heaven (6:19-21).

(5) You see in two directions—your outlook is divided (6:22-23).

(6) You are trying to be loyal in two directions—trying to serve God and mammon (6:24).

(7) You are anxious in two directions—toward what you shall eat and drink and be clothed with, and also toward the kingdom of God (6:25-34).

(8) You are criticizing in two directions—toward your sister or brother with rather heavy emphasis and toward yourself rather lightly (7:1-5).

(9) You are giving yourself—giving yourself to God and also giving that holy thing called personality to the dogs of appetite and the swine of desire (7:6).

In the teaching on prayer, Jesus first pointed out the human temptation to yield to divided loyalties. Prayer ostensibly spoken to God may go unheard, because it really is meant to impress others. Jesus' solution to that temptation was prayer in the closet.

It is ironic that the model prayer that Jesus gave following this advice to pray without ostentation has been spoken or sung in public more often than any other. The Lord's Prayer is sung at weddings and appears often in liturgies. In older patterns of Mennonite worship it was used every Sunday. A minister would lead in prayer and close it with words I heard hundreds of times: "Now let us say with our Lord, 'Our Father. . . .' " The opening words are so gripping that for centuries the prayer has been called the *paternoster* (Latin for "Our Father").

Jesus uses the phrase *in my name* three times in the Gospel of John (14:13; 15:16; 16:23). *In Jesus' name* has been added to so many prayers that it now has the impact of an cliché. The Lord's Prayer is a model for prayer in Christ's name. Although the phrase is not included, it is implicit in the prayer.

The prayer is in two parts, focusing on (1) God and God's purpose and (2) human needs. The organization is noteworthy. Prayer for the realization of God's glory and God's kingdom precedes all other requests. The order in the prayer makes our needs subordinate to God's sovereign purpose of establishing God's kingdom on earth. That surrender of our needs to what God wants to accomplish is what causes prayer to be in Christ's name. An accurate assessment of our needs depends on bringing them under the umbrella of God's intentions for the kingdom. Jesus was totally devoted to doing God's will. When we join Jesus and our motives become like his, then we pray in his name.

If the organization of the Lord's Prayer is instructive, then what are we to make of the fact that Jesus picked one request out of the prayer and underscored it by repetition? Jesus' recapitulation of the forgiveness part of the prayer indicates that he viewed our situation this way: Because we need God to forgive us, we need to forgive others. It is extraordinarily difficult for us to accept the fact that our relationship to God and our relationships to each other are inextricably bound together.

It is startling to contemplate what our situation becomes if we are unforgiving. Essentially we are isolated and alienated, because being unforgiving separates us from God and our sisters and brothers—except those we like and with whom we never disagree. First John is helpful in understanding this: "God is love. Whoever lives in love lives in God, and God in him. . . . We love because [God] first loved us. If anyone says, 'I love God,' yet hates his brother, he is a liar. For anyone who does not love his brother, whom he has seen, cannot love God, whom he has not seen. And he has given us this command: Whoever loves God must also love his brother" (4:16, 19-21).

There are no shortcuts to the goal of personal healing and integration. Wholeness is found by the principles Jesus taught or it is not found at all. The foundation on which wholeness rests is the confession of personal need. On that basis we receive forgiveness and can forgive others.

Application to Life

1. Regarding your motives in prayer—have you learned the value of "closet prayers"? Have you been liberated from wanting to be heard? Is your mind single or is it double?

2. In what ways have you subordinated your need for bread—for material things—to the purposes of God? What is the value of belonging to something that transcends the material?

3. Is your need for forgiveness greater or less than that of others?

Additional Study Resources
Barclay, 190-234; Day, *Autobiography of Prayer;* Driver, 106-16; Jones, 210-13; Jordan, 81-89; Miller, 71-77; Richardson, 'Prayer'; Rinker, *Prayer; IDB* and *ZPEB,* 'Prayer'.

Notes

WHEN YOU FAST, do not look somber as the hypocrites do, for they disfigure their faces to show men they are fasting. I tell you the truth, they have received their reward in full. But when you fast, put oil on your head and wash your face, so that it will not be obvious to men that you are fasting, but only to your Father, who is unseen; and your Father, who sees what is done in secret, will reward you.

Matthew 6:16-18

13

Fasting

MOHANDAS GANDHI practiced the most famous fasting in the twentieth century. His fasts had strong religious overtones and were an effective part of his nonviolent campaign to bring about social, political, and economic change in India. His fasts played a major part in ending British rule over India and in improving conditions for the untouchables, India's low-caste Hindus. Although he remained a Hindu, Gandhi was influenced by Jesus. A worldwide practice since ancient times, fasting is done for a variety of reasons. Gandhi's experience illustrates that fasting has the potential to improve human conditions. In this study we will focus on fasting in the Old Testament, in the teaching of Jesus, and in church history.

Exploring the Text

1. Read 1 Samuel 1:1-20. Why did Hannah fast? What was the outcome of her fasting? What does her experience suggest is the importance of combining fasting and prayer?

2. Read 1 Samuel 20:34. What was Jonathan's reason for fasting? Was there anything religious about his fast?

3. Read 1 Kings 21:1-10; 27-29. What were Ahab's motives for fasting? Was either of his fasts of any spiritual value? What were the

results of the two fasts? Do the results suggest that there is power in fasting?

4. Read 2 Samuel 12:1-23. For what specific occasion did David fast? How did he explain his motives for fasting?

5. Israel had regular times for fasting built into its calendar of sacred events. What value might this have had for them? Might regular times of fasting be valuable for your congregation? Why or why not?

6. Read Isaiah 58:1-7. Why were the people's fasts condemned? What counsel did the Lord offer by which they could redeem their fasting?

7. Read Zechariah 7:1-14. Feasting and fasting are referred to here, and the question of motives is raised. What were the flaws in the people's motives?

8. In Matthew 6:16-18, what does Jesus say was wrong with the motives of some who fasted? What corrective did Jesus offer those who fast? Do you suppose Jesus expected his people to fast?

Is Fasting for Christians?

Jesus' teaching on fasting was the same as his teaching on almsgiving and prayer. Viewed in that way, it makes no more sense for Christians to drop fasting than it would to discontinue prayer and giving to the poor. Jesus approached fasting in the same way that he did other practices of devotion: it was to be done out of a heart that was grateful for God's salvation. It was for God's glory and not to seek the admiration of others, for God looks at the disposition of the heart.

Where I was raised in northern Indiana, neither my church nor my family fasted, though occasionally I heard of Mennonites in Pennsylvania who fasted on Communion Sunday by going without breakfast. More recently, when it became apparent that I was ten to fifteen pounds overweight, I began to fast to lose weight, eating only a piece of fruit or nothing at all for lunch; and the problem pounds melted off. In our weight-conscious culture, it is much more common to fast for appearance and health than for any other reason. While there may not be much spiritual value in fasting for weight loss, I thought it was better to be a trim temple of the Holy Spirit than an overweight one.

Since Jesus' teaching about fasting contains strong words about motives, it seems appropriate to list reasons why people fast. Here are some reasons that appear in the Bible:
- To express devotion to God (Luke 18:9-14)
- To mourn over sin (Jonah 3:5-9)
- To avert disaster (Esther 4:15-16)
- To trap an innocent man (1 Kings 21:9-10)
- To prepare oneself for receiving a revelation (Deuteronomy 9:9-10)
- To face a spiritual crisis, such as Jesus faced during his time in the wilderness (Matthew 4:1-11)
- To make a favorable impression (Matthew 6:16-18)

Here are reasons for fasting that may not appear in the Bible:
- To extend limited food supplies
- As a result of calamities
- To induce mystical experiences, such as dreams and visions
- As an ascetic discipline
- To achieve reforms as Gandhi did, or to gain better treatment as prisoners have done
- To lose weight

Clearly, there are many motives for fasting. Some fasting may not do much good and may not be harmful either. But if the ostensible reason is to be drawn near to God while the real motive is to make a favorable impression, then, like Jesus, we can apply the particularly nasty term *hypocrite.*

Three times in Matthew 6:1-18 Jesus speaks about God in words with profound implications: "Then your Father, who sees what is done in secret, will reward you" (vv. 4, 6, 18). God is near, at hand, always present. That is the perception behind the phrase "your Father, who sees what is done in secret." It is also the perception in Isaiah 11:9, where God's omnipresence is compared to an area covered by water: "For the earth will be full of the knowledge of the Lord as the waters cover the sea."

Jesus' forty-day fast and his teaching about fasting were the prime influences in fasting being a part of the Christian movement from the start. In his practice and teaching it is clear that Jesus did not set fasting aside; and the church has generally so understood him. He assumed that his disciples would fast. All he did, really, was to reiterate the prophets' warnings against superficial and for-malized fasting.

It is significant that Jesus' wilderness fast was viewed later as a precedent for the forty-day penitential fast of Lent. In church his-tory, fasts have fit into three categories: (1) seasonal fasts—during Lent and Advent, for example; (2) weekly fasts, such as no meat on Friday; (3) fasts for solemn occasions, such as baptism, com-munion, and ordination. The three categories were developed by the Catholic Church prior to the Protestant Reformation.

Protestants generally have given far less emphasis to fasting than Catholics have. Catholics have carefully regulated fasting, and they make a distinction between fasting and abstinence, a less severe discipline than fasting. Protestants approach fasting as a more spontaneous and personal option.

What about fasting in the Mennonite Church? Not a word about it appears in the writings of Dirk Philips and Menno Simons, two influential Anabaptist leaders. However, they did encourage sober eating and drinking. A congregation in Amsterdam observed a three-day fast in 1534, ordered by the "prophets and preachers of the church." In colonial Pennsylvania there were spring and fall fasts prior to communion. That practice continued until about 1950; the bishops were the last to drop it. The precommunion fast was carried westward as Mennonites followed the frontier.

Application to Life
1. Now that you have worked through this study on fasting, what is your conclusion about whether fasting should be practiced today?

2. Is there anything in Israel's feast-fast cycle that we should adopt? In our culture, we know how to feast. Should we balance that with fasting?

3. What are the values in fasting? Why do you think Men-nonites and others have discontinued fasting?

Additional Study Resources
Barclay, 234-40; Driver, 116-19; Jones, 213-17; Jordan, 77-80; Richardson, 'Fast, Fasting'; *IDB,* 'Fast, Fasting' and 'Feasts and Fasts'; *ZPEB,* 'Fast, Fasting'; *Mennonite Encyclopedia,* 'Fasting'.

Notes

DO NOT STORE up for yourselves treasures on earth where moth and rust destroy, and where thieves break in and steal. But store up for yourselves treasures in heaven, where moth and rust do not destroy, and where thieves do not break in and steal. For where your treasure is, there your heart will be also.

The eye is the lamp of the body. If your eyes are good, your whole body will be full of light. But if your eyes are bad, your whole body will be full of darkness. If then the light within you is darkness, how great is that darkness!

No one can serve two masters. Either he will hate the one and love the other, or he will be devoted to the one and despise the other. You cannot serve both God and Money.

Therefore I tell you, do not worry about your life, what you will eat or drink; or about your body, what you will wear. Is not life more important than food, and the body more important than clothes? Look at the birds of the air; they do not sow or reap or store away in barns, and yet your heavenly Father feeds them. Are you not much more valuable than they? Who of you by worrying can add a single hour to his life?

And why do you worry about clothes? See how the lilies of the field grow. They do not labor or spin. Yet I tell you that not even Solomon in all his splendor was dressed like one of these. If that is how God clothes the grass of the field, which is here today and tomorrow is thrown into the fire, will he not much more clothe you, O you of little faith? So do not worry, saying, "What shall we eat?" or "What shall we drink?" or "What shall we wear?" For the pagans run after all these things, and your heavenly Father knows that you need them. But seek first his kingdom and his righteousness, and all these things will be given to you as well. Therefore do not worry about tomorrow, for tomorrow will worry about itself. Each day has enough trouble of its own.

Matthew 6:19-34

14

---▲---

Wealth and Worry

WEALTH IS often viewed as the measure of success, the guarantee of security, and the door to happiness. That is a valid viewpoint—but only to a limited extent. I prefer Paul's outlook: "I have learned the secret of being content . . . whether well fed or hungry, whether living in plenty or want" (Philippians 4:12). Somehow it does not seem likely that Paul would have invested money in a state lottery in the hope of winning big.

Success, security, happiness—presumably when one has these, life's worries are over. Depending on how they are defined, we should not knock them. The real question is, How should success, security, and happiness be defined?

Exploring the Text

1. There are three sentences in Matthew 6:19-21. In which verse does Jesus give a basic principle for living? In your own words, what is the principle?

2. How are verses 22-23 related to verses 19-21? Jesus uses metaphors here: the eye, the body, darkness, light. What do the metaphors point to—to our values or to something else?

3. Is verse 24 a follow-up to verses 22-23? If you try to serve two masters, what kind of eye do you have? Regarding the question of serving God or money, what would a good eye be like?

4. One of the problems with wealth is that it can be used as a means of oppression (read James 5:1-6). With his customary vigor, Jesus calls the rich to weep and wail. He gives at least six reasons. Which ones relate to oppression?

5. Read Matthew 6:25-34, Jesus' teaching about worry. Overall, what impression does it make on you? What impresses you most?

6. Three times in this passage Jesus said, "Do not worry" (vv. 25, 31, 34); and he gave seven reasons why we should not worry. Pick out each reason and state it in your own words (vv. 25, 26, 27, 28-30, 32, 33, 34).

Wealth and Christian Faith

One of the problems that goes with ownership of property comes at life's end: whose will it be? In the 1970s property values skyrocketed in our nation, so that many ordinary folk became wealthy. In the Mennonite Church, institutional leaders saw the developing situation as an opportunity and set out to promote estate planning.

Church estate planning is beneficial in more than one way. One, it channels funds to church institutions, whose costs have shot up because of inflation. Two, it relieves the burden that families face in disposing of estates that not uncommonly reach a million dollars. Few families are ready to close such an estate within the parameters of Christian stewardship. Church estate planners could be a valuable asset for such families.

A cartoonist has portrayed a group of greedy-looking relatives, to whom the attorney reads, "I, John Doe, being of sound mind and body, spent it all." Where the family fabric has been torn over a will or the lack of one, the deceased having "spent it all" might have been a better solution. Better yet would be to enter into estate planning and, in the name of the Lord, give where there is need.

Property and wealth are spiritual matters. Anyone who doubts that should read through the Gospel of Luke to see how frequently Jesus raised the issue and what he taught concerning it. In our lesson text Jesus brings together the issues of wealth and worry. We are tempted to believe the notion that wealth ends worry. In over twenty-six years of marriage, Mary and I have learned that acquiring more possessions does not decrease worry.

Here is how Norma Godshall once faced the wealth issue: "Lord, this does not seem to be the day to be looking at finances. I feel overwhelmed, and Dad is at the root of it. Will he be moved today [from Glendale Samaritan Hospital to Glendale Care Center, Glendale, Arizona]? When I look at the picture of the rich, I get angry. I don't even have to look at them. I remember back when Dad gave Mom a mink jacket. I was angry. I thought, 'What a waste of money!' Why was that money not spent on me? After all, I was divorced and needed money for my needs. Lord, I can't even begin to relate to Lazarus. I have never lived that way—I have always been rich. Look at my watch, my rings, my clothing."

In "A Century of Mennonite Quietism (1786-1874)," J. Winfield Fretz says, "Colonial Mennonites brought with them, and kept up, a reputation as industrious and ingenious farmers. Their devotion to long days and hard work in clearing forests and building up their farms, and their minimizing of pleasure and the arts, caused their urban contemporaries and English neighbors to belittle them" (*Gospel Herald,* 28 September 1982). What their contemporaries should have noticed was that embedded in the hard work and care of the land was the realization that land is a gift of God and is to be conserved out of devotion to God. In the long run, that stewardship led to the accumulation of wealth.

There is saying that is common among us: "You can't take it with you." I am never certain just what is meant—hardly that one should live it up so that one has "spent it all" by the time one's life has ended. The Spanish proverb—"Shrouds have no pockets"—is equally ambiguous. Both sayings probably mean that one should have a certain attitude toward possessions—but what attitude? Maybe we are being encouraged to "hang loose." If you have wealth, okay. If not, "don't sweat it."

Jesus was more specific: "Do not store up for yourselves treasures on earth. . . . But store up for yourselves treasures in heaven." A sound interpretation depends on being aware of exactly what Jesus said. The key words used by Jesus are "for yourselves." He did not say, "Do not store up treasures on earth." He said we are not to store up treasures on earth *for ourselves*.

The word *worry* seems a bit anemic in light of all the mischief it causes. The German word *Angst* has much more vigor and is closer to *anxiety*. *Angst* is a profound, unfathomable, and indefinable misgiving about whatever may be in the offing. It often makes people sick. One man developed asthma whenever he heard church bells. The culprit was the stress of being reminded that on his wedding day—when he was already at the church and while the bell rang— he had received the message that his bride-to-be was jilting him.

Worry is one of the stressors that causes people to become ill. Perhaps that is why Paul wrote, "Do not be anxious about anything, but in everything, by prayer and petition, with thanksgiving, present your requests to God. And the peace of God, which transcends all understanding, will guard your hearts and your minds in Christ Jesus" (Philippians 4:6-7).

What an antidote that is for the anxiety that transcends all understanding. In his book *None of These Diseases*, S. I. McMillen says that while our hearts and minds become ill from chronic worry, "the stresses of living are not nearly as responsible for a host of debilitating diseases as are our faulty reactions to those stresses."

Jesus gave seven reasons that we should not worry:

(1) An argument from the value of life (v. 25). Would God give you life and then abandon you?

(2) An argument from the birds (v. 26). Give careful thought to the situation of the birds.

(3) A utilitarian argument (v. 27). Does worry help?

(4) An argument from the flowers (vv. 28-30). How do lilies grow? From the inside outward. The inner person is what counts.

(5) An argument from the pagans (v. 32). What is typical of the pagan mentality is an obsession with material things.

(6) An argument from the nature of God (v. 33). Actually this argument undergirds all the others. These last two reasons for not worrying actually point to ways of overcoming worry.

(7) Another utilitarian argument (v. 34). Which is more useful, to focus on the present or to borrow trouble from the future?

We should consider what an eighteenth-century German philosopher, Immanuel Kant, thought about property. He said that if an individual were alone in the world, the word *mine* would be irrelevant. Therefore, ownership is not a relationship between a person and a thing. Rather, it is a relationship between people, between those who are excluded from property and those to whom possession or use is granted. The right to property is *exclusive*. Where there is no one to exclude, property rights cannot exist.

The following quotes were pulled together by Larry Kehler in "What Mennonites Believe About Money" (Mennonite Publishing House, 1980, p. 7).

When your cattle and sheep, your silver and gold, and all your other possessions have increased, be sure that you do not become proud and forget the Lord your God.
    —*Deuteronomy 8:13, TEV*

Money is like muck, not good unless spread.
    —*Francis Bacon*

Money is a new form of slavery, and distinguishable from the old simply by the fact that it is impersonal—that there is no human relation between master and slave.
    —*Leo N. Tolstoy*

Money can indeed be a servant, but it is a dangerous servant. It is a servant with such amazing potentialities that it requires a master big enough to control it, or else the roles will be reversed. The servant may overthrow the master and take his place. His is the real heart of the problem of personal riches. This is why the New Testament speaks against the accumulation of personal riches. Only God's kingdom and his justice can be a big enough purpose, a worthy enough cause for the final mastering of money.
    —*J. R. Burkholder*

Our wealth is not a handout from God with which we can do as we please. . . . Our wealth was our opportunity. Now it has become our great responsibility. In our money lies our mission to ourselves and to the whole world.
    —*Frank H. Epp*

O Lord, the sin
Done for the things there's money in.
    —*John Masefield*

Because money liberates, our society is so reluctant to see money given to the poor. If we approve welfare at all, we want it to be specified, to be limited, to pay the rent, to allocate food stamps. But not just plain money, no indeed! We justify these limitations by saying that the money might be misused.
    —*J. R. Burkholder*

Perhaps we are guilty of sacrificing leftovers to God. After we have bought everything we went, after we have taken care of ourselves, after we have watched all the TV programs we want, and have gone every place we want to go, if there is anything left over of time or energy or money, we offer this to God.... Try to build into your living standard some sacrifice for the cause of Christ.
    —*John Rudy*

Application to Life

1. Implicit in the lesson text is an amazing perception: life can be full of hope. That is what Jesus' reasons for not worrying add up to. In view of how pervasive worry and *Angst* are, fullness of hope seems improbable. The 6 June 1983 issue of *Time* (in the cover feature, "Stress! Seeking Cures for Modern Anxieties") listed the three best-selling drugs: Tagamet, an ulcer medication; Inderal, a hypertension drug; and Valium, a tranquilizer (p. 48).

   Now that you have studied Jesus' teaching about wealth and worry, which do you think is better, to use the best-selling drugs or Jesus' prescription?

   2. Is there anything about life in our time that invalidates Jesus' teaching about worry?

Additional Study Resources

Bair, *God's Managers;* Barclay, 240-63; Driver, 119-30; Dyck, *Twelve Becoming;* Fairfield, *All That We Are We Give;* Jones, 218-35; Jordan, 90-98; Kehler, *What Mennonites Believe About Money;* McMillen, *None of These Diseases;* Miller, 78-90; *ZPEB*, 'Wealth'.

Notes

_____

_____

_____

_____

_____

_____

_____

_____

_____

_____

_____

_____

_____

_____

_____

_____

_____

_____

_____

_____

_____

_____

_____

_____

_____

_____

_____

*Do NOT JUDGE, or you too will be judged. For in
the same way you judge others, you will be judged, and
with the measure you use, it will be measured to you.*

*Why do you look at the speck of sawdust in your
brother's eye and pay no attention to the plank in your
own eye? How can you say to your brother, "Let me
take the speck out of your eye," when all the time there
is a plank in your own eye? You hypocrite, first take
the plank out of your own eye, and then you will see
clearly to remove the speck from your brother's eye.*

*Do not give dogs what is sacred; do not throw your
pearls to pigs. If you do, they may trample them under
their feet, and then turn and tear you to pieces.*

Matthew 7:1-6

15

——————▲——————

Judging Others

JUDGING OTHERS is a notoriously risky endeavor in light of our limited perception of both ourselves and other people. John Thompson, Georgetown University basketball coach, likes to tell the story of a boy whose father was illiterate and who was doing poorly in school. The boy's mother finally took him to an educator for an evaluation. The educator pointed to objects in his office, and the boy identified them as a radio and a telephone but then froze up, unable to speak. "You shouldn't be embarrassed, because it's not your fault, but this boy is not educable," the educator told the mother. The boy later finished college with a degree in economics and also earned a master's degree in guidance and counseling. The boy was John Thompson.

Exploring the Text

1. In Matthew 7:1-2 Jesus states a principle that governs our lives. What is the principle? How broadly does the principle apply to us? Does it apply in this life only? In the life to come?

2. For a more complete understanding of the principle, study Matthew 6:12, 14-15. Are these verses on the same theme as 7:1-2? What do you think is the difference between the two passages?

3. There is a deliberately overdrawn metaphor in Matthew 7:3-5. What is the impact of the metaphor? How do you feel if you think of yourself with a plank in your eye? Or is that never true of you? Is it always someone else?

4. Do you think Jesus meant to reject all evaluation of other people? What place does giving and receiving counsel have in light of Matthew 7:1-5?

5. To whom was Jesus speaking when he said, "You hypocrite"?

6. Is Paul's statement in Romans 2:1-4 about the same issue as Jesus' statement in Matthew 7:1-5? If you think Paul is interpreting Jesus' teaching, what additional insight does he give?

7. What is the meaning of the phrase "you who pass judgment on someone else" (Romans 2:1)? How do we condemn ourselves when we judge someone else?

8. Is Paul's statement in Romans 2:1 sound psychology? Is it true to life? What does it say about you when another person's conduct irritates you or makes you angry?

9. James 2:1-4 ends with this question: "Have you not discriminated among yourselves and become judges with evil thoughts?" What was the content of these evil thoughts?

10. The scenario in James 2:1-4 is evil. Describe a good counterpart.

11. Read James 2:12-13. Was James reiterating Jesus' teaching in Matthew 7:1-5? What idea is found in James 2:12-13 but not in our lesson text?

12. Some people view James as being severe. Yet he made one of the most heartening statements ever put on paper: "Mercy triumphs over judgment." What are the implications? How does this statement compare with Romans 2:4?

Giving and Receiving Counsel

"Will you give and receive counsel?" That question was traditionally asked of people being baptized and received into membership in Mennonite churches. This custom rested on good intentions, but in practice it fell short of the ideal. The minimum meaning of the question was that every member was to participate in the biannual counsel meetings, usually held on the Sundays prior to communion. That was a formal approach to giving and receiving counsel; and except in small congregations it seemed merely perfunctory, with members responding to a few questions asked by the bishop, such as "Do you have peace with God and man?" and "Is it your desire to have communion?" The form was there but often without the reality of giving and receiving counsel. Now even that form is gone.

Fortunately, many congregations have discovered how to give and receive counsel in other settings. Members' meetings is one setting. Another is the church council meeting, but that is usually only for leadership people. For many years the best setting has been adult Sunday school classes, where people talk to each other about living in faithful obedience to the Lord. Recently some congregations have felt a need for a setting more clearly focused on giving and receiving counsel. They have set up home fellowships, often called small groups or K-groups. People need a close support group of believers, and home fellowships are one way to provide that.

The idea that membership duties include giving and receiving of counsel arises out of a characteristic feature of the Mennonite denomination—the firm belief that the church is a fellowship, a voluntary communion of truly converted believers in Christ who have decided to follow him in full obedience. The impetus for giving and receiving of counsel arises out of two essential aspects of discipleship: (1) dedication to obeying Jesus as Lord, and (2) dedication to the church as a fellowship. Both of these basics of discipleship originate in the teaching of Jesus and the apostles. The text on judging, on removing a speck from another person's eye, deals with how to give and receive counsel so that one does not do more harm than good.

Jesus turned thumbs down on judging. Presumably he meant that *judgmentalism* is unacceptable. Who can stomach a judgmental person anyway? But Jesus did not reject moral discernment. Questions of right and wrong conduct inevitably involve our response to what other people do. Moral discernment also involves how others see what I do. We cannot avoid responding to what people do, but we can avoid going at it with a plank in the eye. Speaking to people about their conduct is delicate business. When we are spoken to about our own conduct, we tense with defensiveness.

It is easy to misjudge other people. When I was fourteen, a young man from our farm community returned from veterinary studies to begin his practice. A farmer who was more vocal than sensible passed this judgment: "He will not last long if he gets any competition." In fact, the veterinarian rose above the competition to become nationally recognized for his expertise.

Jesus' vivid image of eyes with specks in some and planks in others is a reminder of the delicate nature of relationships and how easily feelings are hurt. In 1981 I injured my left eye with a rubber strap I was using to hold down the lid of our car trunk. The strap slipped loose and snapped up right into my eye. The blow was so traumatic that I fell to the ground. After a few minutes I looked into a mirror and saw bad news! The pupil was unnaturally dilated.

Several hours later an ophthalmologist looked into my eye and with a four-letter word confirmed the bad news. He told me that the iris was torn and the lens hung by a thread. Surgery would be necessary—the same procedure as in cataract removal but in this case with complications. "If we are fortunate, you may have a usable eye" was his assessment. Afterward he described the microsurgery. I am glad that he did not have a plank in his eye! As it turned out, his prognosis was too gloomy. The eye healed quickly; and today, with a contact lens, it is nearly equal to the other.

I now thank God with new appreciation for two good eyes. I am also thankful for a skilled ophthalmologist and the precision instruments used to save my eye. The delicate procedures used, it seems to me, must be analogous to the sensitivity that Jesus told us to use in our mutual accountability.

Splendid and resoundingly sensible—that is my response to James' statement about mercy and judgment (James 2:1-13). He does not reject judging in the sense of moral discernment. He condemns it when it is judgmentalism and when it shows favoritism. Human worth is the Creator's gift. It is not dependent on fine clothes or gold rings.

There is some judging that we are obliged to do. We must appraise the character, conduct, and teaching of both ourselves and others. According to 1 Corinthians 6:1-6, we are to judge those inside the church, the world, and angels. Again there is no room for judgmentalism. The evil in judgmentalism is that it sees the wrong in the other person but not in oneself. It sees the other person's flaws but overlooks one's own folly.

Moral and ethical decisions cannot be avoided. We live in a universe based on moral principles, and I do not want my church to be tongue-tied about the following issues:
•anything that devalues and degrades human personality
•the estimated 1.5 million abortions performed annually in the United States
•tax structures that strap the poor but shelter the rich
•rampant militarism.

Nor do I want my congregation to be passive about conditions within the church such as judgmentalism, moral laxity, avoidance of resolving conflict, phony spirituality, false prophets, and excesses of the electronic church. In light of this lesson and out of reverence for the Lord, I want my church to preserve these two things: discipleship as taught in the Sermon on the Mount and awareness that mercy triumphs over judgment.

Application to Life
1. What insights did you gain from this lesson that you believe will be useful in your life?

2. This lesson promotes mutual giving and receiving of counsel. What dangers do you sense in carrying these out? Is it being practiced in your congregation?

3. Are you ever judgmental? What commitment are you making in light of Jesus' teaching about judging?

Additional Study Resources
Augsburger, *Caring Enough to Hear and Be Heard;* Barclay, 264-73; Driver, 132-38; Jones, 243-51; Jordan, 99-107; Miller, 96-102; *ZPEB,*'Judging'; *Mennonite Encyclopedia,* 'Church'.

Notes

_____

_____

_____

_____

_____

_____

_____

_____

_____

_____

_____

_____

_____

_____

_____

_____

_____

_____

_____

_____

_____

_____

_____

_____

_____

_____

ASK AND IT WILL be given to you; seek and you will find; knock and the door will be opened to you. For everyone who asks receives; he who seeks finds; and to him who knocks, the door will be opened.

Which of you, if his son asks for bread, will give him a stone? Or if he asks for a fish, will give him a snake? If you, then, though you are evil, know how to give good gifts to your children, how much more will your Father in heaven give good gifts to those who ask him! In everything, do to others what you would have them do to you, for this sums up the Law and the Prophets.

Matthew 7:7-12

16

Seeking God's Fullness (I)

JESUS DREW a clear connection between what we ask of God and what we receive: "For everyone who asks receives." Could anyone read through the Sermon on the Mount up to this point without realizing a profound sense of personal need? Eleven distinct discipleship issues have been identified so far. The combined weight underscores our need for help in these issues. That may be why Jesus turned to our need at this point. He meant that if we ask for help, we will receive it.

The ask-seek-knock verses will be covered in two lessons. The first focuses on the urgency of recognizing our need; the second on the Holy Spirit, God's answer to our need.

Exploring the Text

1. Immediately preceding the ask-seek-knock verses is the passage about judging others. Jesus said, "You hypocrite, first take the plank our of your own eye." Is there a link between that sentence and the ask-seek-knock statement?

2. Is a plank-eyed person aware of personal need? Whose needs is the plank-eyed person aware of? What would it take to solve the plank-eyed person's problem?

3. If it came down to choosing between Plank-eye and Speck-eye, whom would you rather have for a friend? Explain your choice. Do you feel judgmental in making the choice?

4. If you feel judgmental about the plank-eyes you know, what is your need? In Matthew 7:11 Jesus begins a sentence with "If you, then, though you are evil. . . . " Does that phrase apply to you? How does it fit you? If it does not fit you, explain why.

5. Interpreting the ask-seek-knock passage is not as easy as falling off a log. The preceding study questions and the lesson introduction give one interpretation. Do you agree with it, or does it seem far-fetched? In view of where the passage appears in the Sermon on the Mount, what is the best interpretation?

6. One option is to interpret the ask-seek-knock statement as simply a general word about prayer. Is that your viewpoint? If that is the meaning, why isn't the statement included in the passage on prayer in Matthew 6:5-15?

7. Returning to the view that the ask-seek-knock passage is about our need for God's grace, turn to Luke 18:9-14. Which of the two men in the parable there had come to terms with his need for God's grace? What is the meaning of Jesus' conclusion to the story? In what way was the tax collector's experience an authentication of the ask-seek-knock passage?

8. Coming to terms with our need means recognizing that we need God's grace. That opens the way to finding forgiveness. We also need God's grace to help us be Sermon-on-the-Mount disciples. There are other implications, such as the need for finding emotional, psychological, and physical wholeness. How does acceptance of personal need bring healing?

9. Could anyone live up to the moral-ethical standards of the Sermon on the Mount without help? If not, what help does one need?

Keeping on Pays Off

Jesus uses three imperatives in Matthew 7:7—in English translations, ask, seek, and knock. Something is lost in translation, however; for in the Greek text these imperatives have the force of ongoing action—keep on asking, for example. The dividends are found in persistence. A halfhearted person will ask and then drop the petition. An intensely desirous person will keep on asking, thereby proving the depth of desire and therefore receiving the coveted response.

More than once I have seen a woman finally marry a man because by his persistence he proved to her that he cared. Prayer is effective when the need is intensely felt and does not masquerade behind phony motivation. Prayer is not effective when people simply babble like pagans. In his interpretation of the persistent widow parable, Jesus said, "And will not God bring about justice for his chosen ones, who cry out to him day and night?" (Luke 18:7). However, we should not be so foolish as to think that a certain prayer technique will put a lock on God, that if we do it right, God will be compelled to answer as desired. We pray to our Father, not our robot, in heaven.

In the parable of the Pharisee and the tax collector praying in the temple (Luke 18:9-14), the Pharisee prayed about himself but not about his need, to which he was oblivious. He recognized the tax collector's need but not his own. And he got nowhere in prayer. The tax collector made headway because he was ready to acknowledge his need. He was in touch with reality; the Pharisee was not.

In 1978 Pak Djojo (his full name is Suhadiweko Djojodihardjo), an Indonesian Mennonite leader, spoke at Mennonite World Conference in Wichita, Kansas. In his autobiography, which appears in C. J. Dyck's *Twelve Becoming,* Djojo relates two prayer experiences.

The first took place while he was studying for the ministry. Doubt had overtaken him, and he decided to leave his studies. He said, "Tomorrow I am leaving school for good. The Bible is just not true like my father said it was. I don't even know whether I believe in God anymore. I might as well be honest and admit it." Later he prayed again, "Lord, if you do exist, speak to me. This is the last time I am coming to you."

Late that night Djojo had a vision, during which a voice spoke, "I know what you want to know." Djojo responded, "Who are you? What do you know about me?" And the voice said, "I know what you want to know. Listen. It is this, only this: God loved the world—and you, Djojo—so much that he gave his only Son, that everyone—including you, Djojo—who has faith in him may not die, but have eternal life." Djojo heard himself responding, "Yes, that is what I want to know." When the vision ended, Djojo was changed. He felt free and no longer afraid.

The second experience took place during the disruptions of Indonesia's war for independence from Dutch rule in the late 1940s. Djojo was married and had three children. One day his wife, Armini, told him, "Djojo, there is no food." She had looked everywhere without success. Djojo went to prayer, "Dear God, you have helped us so often. We belong to you. Help us now, I pray, that my family may have food. You know I have nothing left to sell. Help us. Amen."

Armini met Djojo at the door when he returned from the church. She was crying. Someone had brought food.

Pak Djojo's two prayers were very different. But each expressed the need of his life then. In each case God responded to the need. The issue we face in the ask-seek-knock teaching is not so much prayer as it is spiritual need. When Djojo said, "Lord, if you do exist, speak to me. This is the last time I am coming to you," he was recognizing his need for God's help.

The question suggested by Matthew 7:7-12 is this: How can we abide by the high ethical standards in the Sermon on the Mount? Now that we know the Lord's will, isn't our need a source of power to help us be faithful? The church is to be a resource for individuals. But where does the church's strength come from?

Like individuals, the church is sometimes arrogant and forgets that it cannot be a resource without first receiving power. The people of God are always tempted to turn away from their spiritual power source, to despise their birthright and, like Esau, sell it for leftover stew.

In March 1983 the Protestant Health Association held its annual meeting in San Diego. The keynote speaker, Oral Roberts, has put up a hospital in Tulsa, Oklahoma. I was particularly interested in his reason for the hospital: to bring prayer and medicine together. Therefore, the patient is surrounded by a prayer-support group that includes the medical personnel and people from the church. Roberts admitted that they are engaged in an experiment as they try to make medical decisions by both medical diagnosis and spiritual discernment.

There is reason to affirm that approach. The church has tended to forget that medicine does not meet all our health needs. We need to repent of our tendency toward a misplaced trust in medical technology alone and get on with the task of healing the whole person—body, soul, and spirit.

Søren Kierkegaard, a Danish theologian of the nineteenth century, said that if God withdrew from the world, it would not last three seconds. Is the world that dependent on God? While not provable, that is the implication of our biblical theology. Colossians 1:15-17 says that God is the Creator and Sustainer of the universe.

The world is dependent on God. That is how Jesus viewed the human scene. What he does in Matthew 7:7-11 is to offer encouragement: we have a Father who knows our needs and comes through when we ask. The church consists of people who recognize their need, while the world is people who have not yet recognized their need or who have recognized it but have not seen where to go for help. The difference goes even further. Believers recognize their dependence and celebrate the way that God meets their needs. The world has not learned to do that.

Application to Life

1. Where do you stand in regard to your need for God's help? Do you sense any need for comfort, strength, and encouragement from other people? Do you see your own or other people's need more clearly?

2. Do you hear confession of need in your congregation?

3. What is your evaluation of the state of the world? Is the situation deteriorating, improving, or holding steady? Will we survive the twentieth century?

Additional Study Resources

Barclay, 273-81; Driver, 138-42; Dyck, *Twelve Becoming;* Jones, 255-81; Jordan, 108-16; Martin, 47-52; Miller, 102-8.

Notes

So I SAY to you: Ask and it will be given to you; seek and you will find; knock and the door will be opened to you. For everyone who asks receives; he who seeks finds; and to him who knocks, the door will be opened.

Which of you fathers, if your son asks for a fish, will give him a snake instead? Or if he asks for an egg, will give him a scorpion? If you then, though you are evil, know how to give good gifts to your children, how much more will your Father in heaven give the Holy Spirit to those who ask him!

Luke 11:9-13

17

Seeking God's Fullness (II)

THIS IS THE SECOND of two lessons on Jesus' ask-seek-knock saying. The goal of the first lesson was to develop an awareness of our spiritual need—an awareness that without God's grace we are in bad shape. In this lesson the focus is the Holy Spirit, through whom God gives us fullness of life. The Spirit is the solution to our spiritual impoverishment. The Spirit, indispensable to Christians, undergirds the entire range of Christian experience.

The scriptural base for this lesson is the ask-seek-knock saying as it appears in Luke 11:9-13. While in Matthew 7:11 Jesus speaks of the "good gifts" that the Father will give to those who ask him, in Luke 9:13 he is more specific and identifies those good gifts as the Holy Spirit.

Exploring the Text

1. There is more than a hint in the ask-seek-knock saying that God is not stingy. If we, though weak and inadequate, know how to give good gifts, how much more so God, who is not limited by our evil. In light of Jesus' statement, what would you most like to receive from God?

2. Ask, seek, knock—do the three words have equal intensity, or is there a progression in the saying? Do we have to be more insistent as we move on to the next stage? What are the limits to what God will do to meet our need?

3. Luke is explicit where Matthew is general and indicates that the good gift that God gives to those who ask is the Holy Spirit. I once surveyed a group of twenty Christians and asked them how many had ever asked God for the Holy Spirit. None of them had. Did you ever ask? If you did not, can you explain why? If you did, what were the results?

4. While Jesus was praying at his baptism, the Holy Spirit descended on him (Luke 3:21-22). Do you think Jesus asked for the Holy Spirit? What reassurance did the Spirit bring to Jesus (see v. 22b)?

5. The assumption in this lesson is that the "good gifts" in Matthew 7:11 and the Holy Spirit in Luke 11:13 are the same. Is that a valid interpretation? Is it valid to assume that Jesus taught his disciples they needed the Holy Spirit if they were to be able to obey the Sermon on the Mount?

6. Read John 7:37-39. The feast at which Jesus spoke was a commemoration of the event in Exodus 17:1-7, when Moses struck the rock with his staff and water flowed from it. What promise did Jesus make at the feast?

7. What is the living water Jesus spoke of? And what is the requirement for having living water flow from within?

8. Water from the rock at Horeb saved Israel from death by dehydration. Is the water Jesus referred to equally essential? What does it save Jesus' people from?

9. Read Galatians 5:16-25. Verses 16 and 25 use the phrase "live by the Spirit." Would we somehow die without the Spirit, just as Israel would have died without water? Does the rest of the passage give any indication of what it means to live by the Spirit?

10. Ephesians 5:18 commands, "Be filled with the Spirit." How can you obey the command?

Be Filled with the Spirit

The norm for Christians is to be filled with the Spirit. Anything less than that is abnormal. Sometimes it seems as though we get the biblical picture reversed, making the norm abnormal. Could it be that some of us are not up to the norm because we are not thirsty? According to Jesus, the starting place is being thirsty. Is it that we are not asking? Jesus took pains to explain that God goes out of his way to give the Spirit to those who ask him.

Lack of desire, and therefore failure to ask, block the fullness of the Spirit. When the desire for material things captivates us, we ask for those things rather than for the Spirit. E. Stanley Jones (*The Christ of the Mount*, p. 279) says that God may well say no to us when that is the case:

> But this being compelled to say "No" to us is only in the realm of the material. There is one realm in which God does not say "No"—the realm of finding the Spirit. Here everything is open—always! Here we can ask, seek, knock with real assurance. In the most tender words that ever fell from lips Jesus draws the parallel between the human father and the divine, ending with this great climax, "If ye then, being evil, know how to give good gifts unto your children, how much more shall your Father which is in heaven give the Holy Spirit to them that ask him?"

Spiritual poverty results from being isolated and alienated from God. Jesus seemed surprised at the extent of spiritual poverty in people he met. For example, he asked Nicodemus, "You are Israel's teacher, and do you not understand these things?" (John 3:10). Economic poverty was bad enough, but spiritual poverty apparently was worse. Today in North America the picture has improved economically, but it has deteriorated spiritually.

One measure of our situation is the movement worldwide of people into and out of the church. According to David Barrett's *World Christian Encyclopedia* (Oxford University Press, 1982), the Christian church in Africa is growing at a daily rate of 16,000 members, or 5,840,000 annually. Four thousand per day are converting from other religions; 12,000 are added by birth. In contrast, in Europe and North America people are dropping out at a daily rate of 7,600. In 1900 two thirds of the world's Christians lived in Europe and Russia. At present rates of change, by the year 2000 three fifths of them will be in Asia, Africa, and Latin America.

Statistics of that kind give only a partial picture of the state of spirituality. They show Western Christianity in decline but do not show why. Undoubtedly, that spiritual poverty stems from the same inner emptiness that the command "Be filled with the Spirit" intended to correct. The Holy Spirit is God's offer for fullness of life, and that is the direction Jesus was pointing in the ask-seek-knock saying.

People who reside in a desert must adapt to their environment. If they cannot adapt, they must leave or perish. When Moses led the people of Israel out of Egypt, they spent forty years on the Sinai Peninsula, an inhospitable desert. The desert was a training ground, showing the people of Israel how indispensable God's grace is. Only his provision of food and water saved them from extinction. The desert years made an indelible mark on Israel's collective memory.

The region was hostile and infertile, but the experience produced an abundant crop of teaching metaphors. Here is an example from Isaiah 12:2-3:

> The Lord, the Lord, is my strength and my song:
>   he has become my salvation.
> With joy you will draw water
>   from the wells of salvation.

Jesus himself used such a metaphor: "Whoever believes in me . . . streams of living water will flow from within him" (John 7:38). The setting for this statement was the Feast of Tabernacles, or Booths, which was the third of three great annual feasts and commemorated Israel's desert wandering. Each day of the feast a priest would take a pitcher of water from the Pool of Siloam. As he carried the water into the temple, the people recited Isaiah 12:3. The ceremony was a reminder of the time when the Lord saved Israel from death by dehydration in the desert (Exodus 17:1-7).

Jesus used the water-from-the-rock event to proclaim the fulfillment of the promise inherent in the desert incident. "If a man is thirsty, let him come to me and drink," Jesus said on the seventh and climaxing day of the feast (John 7:37). A person can drink that water only in swallows, a little at a time, but the result is streams of living water. By "living water" Jesus meant the Holy Spirit, the solution to our spiritual poverty and the God-given source of fullness of life. Is it at all surprising that Paul alluded to this image when he wrote, "Be filled with the Spirit" (Ephesians 5:18)?

Believers trying to make it on their own are like a desert needing the water of God's grace, the Holy Spirit. They are like Israel in the desert without food or water. Christians live in the world, which is a spiritual wasteland. If they are to maintain any spiritual vitality at all, they need a stream of living water flowing from within them.

In describing the transformation that God accomplishes when a person is changed from barren desert to productive soil, from spiritual poverty to spiritual affluence, Scripture often uses the creation motif. "If anyone is in Christ, he is a new creation" (2 Corinthians 5:17). The picture that emerges is God restoring his creation by renewing us through faith in Jesus Christ. Paul's statement invests the creation story with a new dimension. The understanding is that Jesus came to restore the Creator's original intention. What better way to express it than to say that in Christ we are new creatures.

The optimum realization of the new creation is a person in whom the Spirit of God resides—as in Paul's evocative words, "Do you not know that your body is a temple of the Holy Spirit, who is in you, whom you have received from God?" (1 Corinthians 6:19).

The "new creation" metaphor is rich in meaning. Genesis 1:2 describes the earth as having been formless, empty, and dark—a chaotic, desolate scene unsuited for life. But the Spirit of God hovered over the desolation and brought into existence that which God called "very good." In our lives we once were, and we continue to feel, like a chaotic mess. But over our desolation too the Spirit hovers, bringing into existence a new creation. In the Sermon on the Mount, Jesus referred to the people as being evil. When the Spirit's work is done, may God see us as "very good."

Application to Life

1. Jesus and the apostles taught that we need the Holy Spirit to live a holy life. Jesus said that God is eager to give us the Spirit. Have you taken advantage of the offer? Have you asked God for the Holy Spirit?

2. What is your source of power for life? Have you anything at all that non-Christians do not have? Is it possible to live up to the standards Jesus gave in the Sermon on the Mount without a divine power source?

3. The Sermon on the Mount is for people in the marketplace, in the factory, in the office, on the farm, at home. You cannot take a church support group with you to all those places. Whom can you take along?

Additional Study Resources

Barclay, 264-80; Driver, 138-42; Jones, 255-81; Jordan, 108-14; Miller, 102-6; *IDB* and *ZPEB,* 'Holy Spirit'.

Notes

_____

_____

_____

_____

_____

_____

_____

_____

_____

_____

_____

_____

_____

_____

_____

_____

_____

*E*NTER THROUGH *the narrow gate. For wide is the gate and broad is the road that leads to destruction, and many enter through it. But small is the gate and narrow the road that leads to life, and only a few find it.*

Watch out for false prophets. They come to you in sheep's clothing, but inwardly they are ferocious wolves. By their fruit you will recognize them. Do people pick grapes from thornbushes, or figs from thistles? Likewise every good tree bears good fruit, but a bad tree bears bad fruit. A good tree cannot bear bad fruit, and a bad tree cannot bear good fruit. Every tree that does not bear good fruit is cut down and thrown into the fire. Thus, by their fruit you will recognize them.

Not everyone who says to me, "Lord, Lord," will enter the kingdom of heaven, but only he who does the will of my Father who is in heaven. Many will say to me on that day, "Lord, Lord, did we not prophesy in your name, and in your name drive out demons and perform many miracles?" Then I will tell them plainly, "I never knew you. Away from me, you evildoers!"

Therefore everyone who hears these words of mine and puts them into practice is like a wise man who built his house on the rock. The rain came down, the streams rose, and the winds blew and beat against that house; yet it did not fall, because it had its foundation on the rock. But everyone who hears these words of mine and does not put them into practice is like a foolish man who built his house on sand. The rain came down, the streams rose, and the winds blew and beat against that house, and it fell with a great crash.

Matthew 7:13-27

18

Decision Time

GOOD SERMONS usually end with a call to commitment, and that is how Jesus ended his. Matthew 7:13-27 has three points: (1) life offers two roads; we must choose which one we will travel; (2) those who choose the Jesus way will face dangers along the way; and (3) if our life project is going to last, it can do so only if it rests on Jesus' word.

In concluding this study of the Sermon on the Mount it is appropriate to review the structure of the sermon:

A. The character of Jesus' people (5:1-20).

B. How his people relate to each other (5:21-48).

C. How his people relate to God (6:1-34).

D. Two responses to the Sermon's ethical standards:
   1. When others do not measure up (7:1-6).
   2. When I don't measure up (7:7-12).
   3. Jesus' call to commitment (7:13-27).

Exploring the Text

1. In Matthew 7:13-14 it is clear that Jesus calls people to make a choice. What options does he offer? To whom is the call given? At what point in life's journey is the call pertinent? Is it a call to faith, or what is it?

2. Jesus pointed out that each of the two roads has a destination. One is destruction. What does that mean? The other destination is life. What does that mean? Are they this-worldly destinies or otherworldly or both?

3. Matthew 7:15-23 has two warnings, each about dangers along the way. The first one is a warning against false prophets. Who are false prophets and what danger do they bring?

4. Who do you think are today's "ferocious wolves"? Are there fellow travelers who are a deadly menace? For additional biblical information about false prophets, see 2 Peter 2:1-3. What are the deeds and attitudes of false prophets?

5. The second warning is against those whose "Lord, Lord" is counterfeit. Who are these people? Are they the false prophets or someone else? What danger are they to Jesus' people?

6. What are the things that the "Lord, Lord" people say and do which appear to be good but will not avail "on that day"? How can anyone do those things under false pretenses?

7. Jesus said that we can recognize false prophets by their fruit. What is the difference between good fruit and bad fruit?

8. Does the good-fruit-bad-fruit test also apply to the smooth-talking "Lord, Lord" set? What is bad fruit in that case? Is it perhaps loving the spectacular—prophecy, exorcism, miracles—and despising simple obedience?

9. Read Matthew 7:24-27. The fakers and the faithful will each get a suitable reward, which Jesus described as a crash for one and survival for the other. When will that time of maximum stress hit us? What will it consist of?

10. Practicing Jesus' teaching is the crucial issue. Do the big talkers and "ferocious wolves" practice Jesus' teaching? Is putting the Sermon on the Mount into practice the good fruit of Matthew 7:16-20?

Practicing Jesus' Teaching

Biologically, life has a starting point and an end. The start is birth; the end is death. That is the way it is, and no human can do anything to alter that reality. However, there are other factors that can be altered, and that is what Jesus referred to when he spoke of the broad and narrow roads. We can choose which road we take. We are creatures of choice, which means that we have something to say about the quality of our lives.

Jesus departed from biological facts when he spoke of choosing which road we will travel on. The choice is the start of a journey, and the journey has a destination that is determined by the road a person chooses to follow. This makes the choice exceedingly important. The quality of the journey is also significant. The journey begins at two gates: a small gate and a narrow road, or a wide gate and a broad road.

With the ability to evaluate the consequences, choosing is a uniquely human privilege. Choice, with its fateful potential, has a gripping fascination. We can estimate the results, but we cannot remove the mystery of the unknown. Choice makes us vulnerable. Choice makes us human. Choice can take us to God. Choice can take us away from God.

Sometimes it is helpful to see the choices that Christians in other cultures have to make. Ngongo David is a leader in the Evangelical Mennonite Church in Zaire, Africa. His choices illustrate Jesus' word about making a start. As a young man he heard a missionary preach about how the Holy Spirit spoke to Paul on the Damascus road. Ngongo David later wrote, "I felt the Spirit speaking to me, too, and I said 'yes' to God."

Subsequently Ngongo David married Mitoro Ruth, also a Christian. He wrote, "Ours was the first Christian wedding in Nyanga. Our marriage certificate says that I would not beat Mitoro as a non-Christian husband does. I would eat with her, when at home, which he does not. A non-Christian man is the master in his house and eats by himself. His wife eats with the children in the kitchen. He treats his wife like a servant-slave, but Mitoro and I were partners together for God" (C. J. Dyck, *Twelve Becoming*).

The narrow gate and narrow road suggest the discipline required of anyone choosing to follow Jesus as Lord. Obedience is not easy. It is made even more difficult by the dangers that narrow-road travelers face. Sometimes the seductive thought comes that serving the Lord should mean the end of struggle. Why can't we simply "snuggle up to each other" and with the Lord's protection let the world go by? Jesus said the narrow way is the best solution, not the easiest.

The dangers along the narrow way require us to discern between the true and the false. To do that we need the gift of the Holy Spirit that Paul calls "the ability to distinguish between spirits" (1 Corinthians 12:10). The church constantly faces issues that require us to discern what is the narrow way. In recent years the "gospel of health and wealth" has become such an issue. It has gained tremendous popularity in North America. People saying "Lord, Lord" give this message:

Sickness is not God's will; health is.
Therefore, Christians should always be healthy.
Poverty is not God's will; wealth is.
Therefore, we should all be wealthy.

One way to test an interpretation of Scripture is to ask whether it can be universalized. Would it make sense in other parts of the world? The gospel of health and wealth would not make sense in the world's poor nations. It is a product of affluent North America.

The health-and-wealth gospel assumes that there are unlimited resources on planet Earth. Therefore, we are faced with two issues: biblical interpretation and the use of the earth's resources. How should we view our planet and the future of humankind?

Early in the 1970s the outlook was often optimistic. It was articulated by Herman Khan, director of the Hudson Institute, in an address given at the Futures Conference in 1971. He said the rich would get richer and their wealth would help the poor as well. A year later D. L. Meadows and D. H. Meadows—in *The Limits to Growth: A Report of the Club of Rome's Project on the Predicament of Mankind* (New York: Universe Books, 1972)—concluded that unless drastic changes are made, the world cannot survive beyond the year 2025. Since then the debate has continued with a proliferation of books, articles, and speeches. For a fuller description of the debate you may wish to read "Awakening from the Western Dream—A World in Trauma," chapter 2 of Tom Sine's book *The Mustard Seed Conspiracy*.

Which worldview should we adopt? We need to choose, bearing in mind that the choice will do much to determine our definition of discipleship. If there are unlimited resources, then we can look more favorably at the gospel of health and wealth. If we acknowledge that many resources are nonrenewable and are being rapidly depleted, then under Jesus' lordship we can make an appropriate response.

Tom Sine took the pessimistic worldview but then turned it into an appeal for positive action in accord with the gospel of Christ. Sine says it is the Lord's will to equalize wealth. "God placed enough resources on this planet for everyone to live decently, but not for everyone to live like Americans . . . not even Americans" (p. 31). But the answer for the world lies in the mustard seed, meaning in the hearts of believers who are ready to tighten their belts and share.

It seems to me that at the end of his sermon Jesus looked back over what he had taught and then said: "It's decision-making time. I invite you to begin the journey that leads to life. The starting place is a choice between a small gate and one too wide to miss.

"Even when you are on the right road, watch out for seducers and sweet talkers who speak right but live wrong, omitting justice, mercy, and love from their lifestyle.

"The world is full of seductive words, but mine are basic. They make the difference between success and failure. Envision life as house-building. A house standing on my word will never topple. You are a builder. Whether or not to build is not an option. The option is, Where will you build? There is no getting around it.

"If you build on my Word your building will stand. Everyone who hears these words of mine and puts them into practice is like a wise man."

Application to Life

1. Life stories are fascinating. Each one of us has a story. At some point in life, one should be able to begin his or her story by saying, "I thank Jesus Christ for my story." Have you done that? Can you do it?

2. The Sermon on the Mount outlined a way to live. When Jesus finished, he said, in effect, "There are two roads to choose from: the Sermon-on-the-Mount road or the world's road. Choose the Sermon-on-the-Mount one." How does Jesus' invitation make you feel? Can you make such a weighty choice?

Additional Study Resources

Barclay, 281-97; Driver, 142-53; Dyck, 89-95; Jones, 282-332; Jordan, 114-26; Miller, 109-21; Sine, *Mustard Seed Conspiracy.*

Notes

The Author

Jason Martin is pastor of Pleasant View Mennonite Church, Goshen, Indiana, and serves as overseer for seven congregations in northern Indiana. He also has served as pastor at Trinity Mennonite Church in Phoenix, Arizona, and at Wawasee Lakeside Chapel and Olive Mennonite Church, both in northern Indiana.

Jason is a graduate of Goshen College and of Goshen Biblical Seminary. He also has an M.A. in Spanish from the University of Notre Dame. He taught Spanish in public high school for eight years.

Other books that Jason has written include *The Holy Spirit in the Life of the Church* and *The People of God in Community*. He has also written curriculum materials for The Foundation Series and the Uniform Series.

Jason and his wife, Mary, raised a family of four children.